Norton Anthology of Western Music
In two volumes

Volume II:

Classic · Romantic · Modern

NORTON ANTHOLOGY
OF WESTERN MUSIC

In Two Volumes

VOLUME II

Classic · Romantic · Modern

Edited by Claude V. Palisca

YALE UNIVERSITY

W · W · NORTON & COMPANY

NEW YORK · LONDON

Copyright © 1980 by W. W. Norton & Company, Inc.
Published simultaneously in Canada by George J. McLeod Limited, Toronto.
Printed in the United States of America.

First Edition

Library of Congress Cataloging in Publication Data
Main entry under title:
Norton anthology of western music.
    Includes indexes.
    CONTENTS: v. 1. Medieval, Renaissance, baroque.—
v. 2. Classic, romantic, modern.
    1. Vocal music.   2. Instrumental music.   I. Palisca,
Claude V.
M1N825   [M1495]   [M5]   780.8'2   80–11916
ISBN 0–393–95143–X (v. 1)
ISBN 0–393–95151–0 (v. 2)
    2 3 4 5 6 7 8 9 0

To J., C., and M.

Contents

CONCERTO

OPERA AND CANTATA

ROMANTIC

PIANO MUSIC

Contents

Orchestral Music

Chamber Music

Lied

Opera

Choral Music

MODERN

OPERA

Preface

The title of this anthology lacks one important qualifier: it is a *historical* anthology of western music. There is a wide difference between a historical anthology and one intended simply to supply a selection of music for study and analysis.

A historian cannot confine himself to studying in splendid isolation the works that are the usual stuff of anthologies. He is interested in products of the imagination great and small as they exist in a continuum of such works. Just as composers did not create in a musical void, standing aloof from the models of their predecessors and contemporaries, so the historically-oriented student and analyst must have the primary material that permits establishing historical connections. This anthology invites students and teachers to make such connections. It confronts, for example, important works and their models, pieces written on a common subject or built according to similar procedures or that give evidence of subtle influences of one composer's work on another's.

Most music before 1500 was composed on some pre-existent music, and there are numerous examples of this practice even after that date. Whenever possible in this anthology, the music that served to ignite a composer's imagination is provided. In one notable case a single chant gave rise to a chain of polyphonic elaborations. This is the Alleluia with verse, *Alleluia Pascha nostrum* (NAWM 13), elaborated by Leonin in organum purum with clausulae, refreshed with substitute clausulae by his successors; and both his and the new clausulae were turned into motets by adapting Latin or French texts to them or made fuller with new parts both with and without texts. (This Alleluia set, although different in content, format and realization, is itself modeled on similar sets on this chant devised by Richard Crocker and Karl Kroeger as local teaching aids, and I am indebted to them for the general idea and certain details).

A similar chain of works are the masses built upon the melisma on the word *caput* in the Sarum version of the Antiphon, *Venit ad Petrum:* three are here given, the first possibly by Dufay, the second by Obrecht, and the third by Ockeghem, each in turn influencing the next (NAWM 35, 36, and 37). It is instructive similarly to observe in Josquin's early motet, *Tu solus, qui facis mirabilia* (NAWM 29), the way he absorbed fragments of Ockeghem's arrangement of the song, *D'ung aultre amer* (NAWM 44), or to be able to refer to the *Benedictus* of Taverner's Mass, *Gloria tibi trinitas* (NAWM 38), the source of the famous subject, *In nomine,* when studying one of the many variations upon it, that by Christopher Tye (NAWM 61). The process of coloration and variation that produced Luys de Narváez's arrangement for vihuela (NAWM 45b) may be inferred from comparing it to the original polyphonic chanson *Mille regretz* by Josquin (NAWM 45a). A later example of this process, starting with a monodic model, may be found in the *Lachrimae* pavans of Dowland, Byrd, Farnaby, and Sweelinck (NAWM 98a, b, c, and d) based on the well-known air, *Flow my tears,* by Dowland (NAWM 66). In the twentieth century the variation procedure is the structural principle for several excerpts, namely those by Strauss (NAWM 142), Schoenberg (NAWM 145), and Copland (NAWM 147). Arcadelt's parody in his Mass (NAWM 39) of Mouton's motet, *Noe, noe* (NAWM 31) may be assumed to be a tribute, but what of Handel's similar recycling of Urio's *Te Deum* (NAWM 86) in *Saul* (NAWM 87)?

More subtle connections may be detected between Lully's overture to *Armide* (No. 73a) and the opening chorus of Bach's cantata, *Nun komm, der Heiden Heiland* (NAWM 88), between Gossec's *Marche lugubre* (NAWM 113) and the Funeral March from Beethoven's "Eroica" Symphony (NAWM 114), between the nocturnes of Field and Chopin (NAWM 121 and 122), or between Mussorgsky's song *Les jours de fête* (NAWM 154) and Debussy's *Nuages* (NAWM 140).

Comparison of the musical realization of the same dramatic moments in the legend of Orpheus by Peri and Monteverdi (NAWM 68 and 69) reveal the latter's debts to the former. Again, two orchestral comentaries on the Queen Mab speech in *Romeo and Juliet* highlight the distinct gifts of Berlioz (NAWM 125) and Mendelssohn (NAWM 126) as tone poets. It is revealing to compare the settings of Mignon's song from Goethe's *Wilhelm Meister* by Schubert, Schumann and Wolf (NAWM 129, 130, and 131), or Grandi and Schütz in their respective versions of a text from the *Song of Songs* (NAWM 82 and 84).

Some of the selections betray foreign influences, as the penetration of Italian styles in England in Purcell's songs for *The Fairy Queen* (NAWM 74) or Humfrey's verse and anthem (NAWM 85). The crisis in Handel's career, brought on partly by the popularity of the ballad opera and by the English audience's rejection of his own Italian *opera seria,* is documented in a scene from *The Beggar's Opera* (NAWM 78) and by the changes within his own dramatic *oeuvre* (NAWM 77, 79 and 87). The new Italian style to which he also reacted is exemplified by Pergolesi's felicitous cantata on the Orpheus myth (NAWM 117).

Some composers are represented by more than one work to permit comparison of early and late styles—Josquin, Monteverdi, Bach, Handel, Vivaldi, Haydn, Beethoven, Liszt, Schoenberg, Stravinsky—or to show diverse approaches by a single composer to distinct genres—Machaut, Dufay, Ockeghem, Arcadelt, Willaert, Monteverdi, Bach, Mozart.

A number of the pieces marked new departures in their day, for example Adrian Willaert's *Aspro core* from his *Musica nova* (NAWM 52), Nicola Vicentino's chromatic *Laura che'l verde lauro* (NAWM 54), Viadana's solo concerto, *O Domine Jesu Christe* (NAWM 81), Rousseau's scene from *Le devin du village* (NAWM 118), or C. P. E. Bach's sonata (NAWM 104). Other pieces were chosen particularly because they were singled out by contemporary critics, such as Arcadelt's *Ahime, dov'è 'l bel viso* (NAWM 51), hailed in 1549 by Bishop Cirillo Franco as a ray of hope for the future of text-expressive music; or Monteverdi's *Cruda Amarilli* (NAWM 64), dismembered by Artusi in his dialogue of 1600 that is at once a critique and a defense of Monteverdi's innovations; Caccini's *Perfidissimo volto* (NAWM 63), mentioned in the preface to his own *Euridice* as one of his pioneering attempts, or Cesti's *Intorno all'idol mio* (NAWM 72), one of the most cited arias of the mid-seventeenth century. Others are Lully's monologue in *Armide, Enfin il est en ma puissance* (NAWM 73b), which was roundly criticized by Rousseau and carefully analyzed by Rameau and d'Alembert; the scene of Carissimi's *Jephte* (NAWM 83), singled out by Athanasius Kircher as a triumph of the powers of musical expression; and the *Danse des Adolescentes* in Stravinsky's *Le Sacre* (NAWM 143), the object of a critical uproar after its premiere.

Certain of the items serve to correct commonplace misconceptions about the history of music. Cavalieri's *Dalle più alte sfere* (NAWM 67) of 1589 shows that florid monody existed well before 1600. The movements from Clementi's and Dussek's sonatas (NAWM 105 and 106) reveal an intense romanticism and an exploitation of the piano that surpass Beethoven's writing of the same period and probably influenced it. The movement from Richter's String Quartet (NAWM 107) tends to refute Haydn's paternity of the genre. Sammartini's and Stamitz's symphonic movements (NAWM 109 and 110) show that there was more than one path to the Viennese symphony. The Allegro from Johann Christian Bach's E flat Harpsichord Concerto testifies to Mozart's (NAWM 116) dependence on this earlier model. The scene from Meyerbeer's *Les Huguenots* (NAWM 135) is another seminal work that left a trail of imitations.

Most of the selections, however, are free of any insinuations on the part of this editor. They are simply typical, superlative creations that represent their makers, genres, or times outstandingly. Most of the *Ars nova* and many of the Renaissance works are in this category, as are a majority of those of the Baroque, Romantic, and Modern periods. My choices mark important turning points and shifts of style, historical phenomena that are interesting if not always productive of great music, new models of constructive procedures, typical moments in the work of individual composers, and always challenging exemplars for historical and structural analysis.

The proportion of space assigned to a composer or work is not a reflection of my estimation of his greatness, and, regretfully, numerous major figures could not be represented at all. In an anthology of limited size every work chosen excludes another of corresponding size that is equally worthy. Didactic functionality, historical illumination, intrinsic musical quality rather than "greatness" or "genius" were the major criteria for selection.

The inclusion of a complete Office (NAWM 2) and a nearly complete Mass (NAWM 1) deserves special comment. I realize that the rituals as represented here have little validity as historical documents of the Middle Ages. It would have been more authentic, perhaps, to present a mass and office as practiced in a particular place at a particular moment, say in the twelfth century. Since the Vatican Council, the liturgies printed here are themselves archaic formulas, but that fact strenghens the case for their inclusion, for opportunities to experience a Vespers service or Mass sung in Latin in their classic formulations are rare indeed. I decided to reproduce the editions of the modern chant books, with their stylized neumatic notation, despite the fact that they are not *urtexts,* because these books are the only resources many students will have available for this repertory, and it should be part of their training to become familiar with the editorial conventions of the Solesmes editions.

These volumes of music do not contain any commentaries, because only an extended essay would have done justice to each of the selections. By leaving interpretation to students and teachers, I hope to enrich their opportunities for research and analysis, for discovery and appreciation. Another reason for not accompanying the music with critical and analytical notes is that this anthology was conceived as a companion to Donald J. Grout's *A History of Western Music,* as revised with my participation in this classic text's Third Edition. Brief discussions of almost every number in this collection will be found in that book: some barely scratch the surface, others are extended analytical and historical reflections. An index to these discussions by number in this anthology is at the back of each volume.

The anthology, it must be emphasized, was intended to stand by itself as a selection of music representing every important trend, genre, national school and historical development or innovation.

The translations of the poetic and prose texts are my own except where acknowledged. They are literal to a fault, corresponding to the original line by line, if not word for word, with consequent inevitable damage to the English style. I felt that the musical analyst prefers precise detail concerning the text that the composer had before him rather than imaginative and evocative writing. I am indebted to Ann Walters for helping with some stubborn medieval Latin poems and to Ingeborg Glier for casting light on what seemed to me some impenetrable lines of middle-high German.

A number of research assistants, all at one time students at Yale, shared in the background research, in many of the routine tasks, as well as in some of the joys of discovery and critical selection. Robert Ford and Carolyn Abbate explored options in pre-Baroque and post-Classical music respectively during the selection phase. Gail Hilson and Kenneth Suzuki surveyed the literature on a sizeable number of the items, while Susan Cox Carlson contributed her expertise in early polyphony. Clara Marvin assisted in manifold ways in the last stages of this compilation.

My colleagues at Yale were generous with their advice on selections, particularly Elizabeth Keitel on Machaut, Craig Wright on Dufay, Leon Plantinga on Clementi, John Kirkpatrick on Ives, and Allen Forte on Schoenberg. Leeman Perkins' and Edward Roesner's suggestions after seeing preliminary drafts of the Medieval and Renaissance sections contributed to rounding out those repertories. I am also indebted to Paul Henry Lang for his reactions to the classic period choices and to Christoph Wolff for those of the Baroque period.

The Yale Music Library was the indispensable base of operations, and its staff a prime resource for the development of this anthology. I wish to thank particularly Harold Samuel, Music Librarian, and his associates Alfred B. Kuhn, Kathleen J. Moretto, Karl W. Schrom, Kathryn R. Mansi, and Warren E. Call for their many favors to me and my assistants.

Most of all I have to thank Claire Brook, whose idea it was to compile an anthology to accompany the Third Edition of *A History of Western Music.* Her foresight, intuition, and creative editorial style gave me confidence that somehow within a short space of time this complex enterprise would unfold. Thanks to the quotidian efforts of her assistant, Elizabeth Davis, who with remarkable efficiency and insight steered the project through a maze of production pitfalls, we were able to achieve the goal of bringing out this anthology and text together.

Professor Grout's text set a standard of quality and scope that was my constant challenge and inspiration. For his enthusiastic acceptance of the project, his cooperation, and his willingness to subordinate proprietary and justly prideful feelings to a pedagogical ideal of historical text-*cum*-anthology, the users of these tools and I owe a great debt, particularly if this coupling achieves a measure of the success that his book has enjoyed.

W. W. Norton and I are grateful to the individuals and publishers cited in the footnotes for permission to reprint, re-edit or adapt material under copyright. Where no modern publication is cited, the music was edited from original sources.

Finally, to my wife Jane, and my son and daughter, Carl and Madeline, to whom this anthology is dedicated with affection, I must express my gratitude for patiently enduring the deprivations, hibernations, even estivations, over the years of gestation required by this and the companion work.

Claude V. Palisca
Branford, Connecticut

Norton Anthology of Western Music
In two volumes

Volume II:

Classic · Romantic · Modern

Domenico Scarlatti *(1685–1757)*
Sonata in D Major, K. 119 (1749)

103

il primo tempo

Carl Philipp Emanuel Bach (*1714–88*)
Sonata IV in A Major, Wq. 55/IV:
Poco adagio (second movement)

104

C. P. E. Bach, *Sechs Clavier-Sonaten für Kenner und Liebhaber* (Leipzig, 1779). Bach's sonatas are identified by the numbers in Alfred Wotquenne, *Thematisches Verzeichnis der Werke Ph. E. Bachs* (Leipzig, 1905). Reprinted from *Sechs Claviersonaten: Erste Sammlung*, edited by Lothar Hoffmann-Erbrecht (Leipzig, n.d.), pp. 24–36.

105

Muzio Clementi *(1752–1832)*
Sonata in G Minor, Opus 34, No. 2
(1795): Largo e' sostenuto—Allegro con fuoco (first movement)

Reprinted from *Deux grandes Sonates pour Clavecin ou Forté-Piano, Oeuvres trente-quatre ou trente-huit,* (Paris, Sieber, 180-).

106   Jan Dussek (1760–1812)
Sonata in E flat, Opus 44, ''Les Adieux'' (*pub. 1800*): Grave—Allegro moderato (first movement)

Reprinted from *Sonatas for Piano*, edited by Jan Racek and Václan Jan Sýkora, Vol. III (Prague, 1962), pp. 20–50.
Reprinted by permission.

*) orig.

*) sempre orig. divisione di Dusik

*) orig.:

Franz Xaver Richter (*1709–89*)
String Quartet in B-flat Major, Opus 5, No. 2 (*1768*): Fugato presto (third movement)

107

Reprinted from *Denkmäler deutscher Tonkunst,* Series 2: *Denkmäler der Tonkunst in Bayern.* Jahrg. 15, Vol. I, edited by Hugo Riemann (Leipzig, 1914), pp. 18–21. Reprinted by permission of Breitkopf & Härtel, Wiesbaden.

Ludwig van Beethoven (1770–1827)
String Quartet in C-sharp Minor, No. 14, Opus 131 (1826)

108

a) *Adagio ma non troppo e molto espressivo* (*first movement*)

Complete String Quartets (New York: Dover, 1975), pp. 119–26, reprinted from the Breitkopf & Härtel *Complete Works* Edition (Leipzig, n.d.)

4 (122)

b) *Allegro molto vivace (second movement)*

Giovanni Battista Sammartini
(1700/01–75)
Symphony in F Major, No. 32 *(before 1744)*: Allegro (first movement)

109

The symphonies are identified through the numbering in Newell Jenkins and Bathia Churgin, *Thematic Catalogue of the Works of Giovanni Battista Sammartini* (Cambridge: Harvard University Press for the American Musicological Society, 1976). Reprinted by permission of the publishers from *The Symphonies of G. B. Sammartini*, Vol. I: *The Early Symphonies*, edited by Bathia Churgin (Harvard Publications in Music, 2). Cambridge, Mass.: Harvard University Press, © 1968 by the President and Fellows of Harvard College.

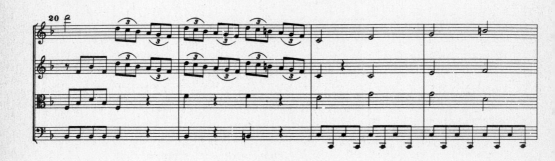

*m. 35: In mm. 35-36, the octave skips in the manuscript are reversed, starting with the upper octave and descending.

110

Johann Anton Wenzel Stamitz (1717–57)
Sinfonia a 8 in E-flat Major (*La Melodia Germanica* No. 3)(1754–55): Allegro assai (first movement)

Denkmäler deutscher Tonkunst, Series 2: *Denkmäler der Tonkunst in Bayern*. Jahrg. 7, Vol. II (Leipzig, 1906), pp. 1–12.
Reprinted by permission of Broude Brothers Limited.

Franz Joseph Haydn (1732–1809)
Symphony No. 7 in C Major, "Midi"
(Hoboken I:7; 1761)

111

a) *Adagio-Allegro* (*first movement*)

The numbering of Haydn's symphonies follows A. von Hoboken's *Thematisches-bibliographisches Werkverzeichnis* (Mainz, 1957, 1971). Reprinted from *Joseph Haydn, Critical Edition of the Complete Symphonies*, edited by H. C. Robbins Landon, Vol. I, pp. 157–80. Reprinted by permission of Ludwig Doblinger (B. Herzmansky), Vienna.

*) Esterházy · Archiv

*) Ausführung / *execution*

112

Franz Joseph Haydn
Symphony No. 77 in B-flat Major
(Hoboken I: 77; 1782): Finale, Allegro
spiritoso (fourth movement)

For an explanation of the numbering see page 51. Reprinted from *Ibid.*, Vol. 8 (Vienna, 1966), pp. 188–203.

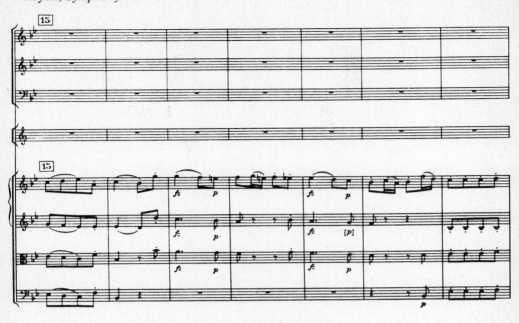

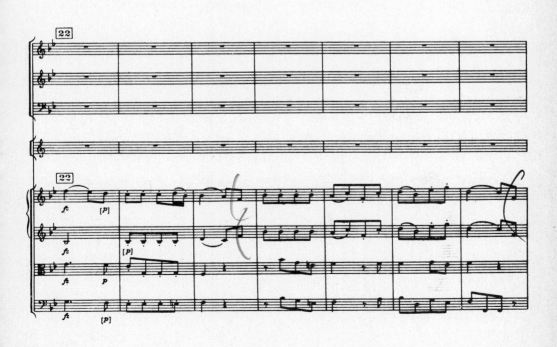

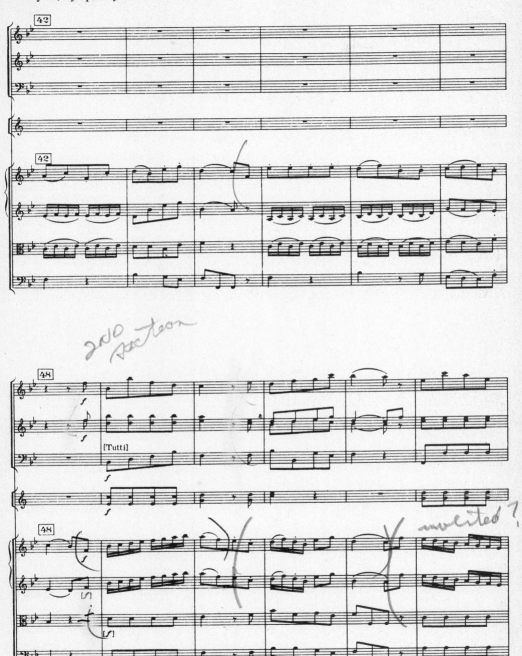

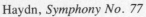

*)Pausen| in Esterházy-Archiv
Rests }

113

François Joseph Gossec (*1734–1829*)
Marche lugubre (*1790*)

Scored from printed parts in Paris, B. N., Dépt. de la Musique.

Ludwig van Beethoven
Symphony No. 3 in E-flat Major,
"Eroica" *(1803–1804): Marcia funebre*
(second movement)

115

Johann Christian Bach (1735–82)
Concerto for Harpsichord or Piano and Strings in E-flat Major, Opus 7, No. 5: Allegro di molto (first movement)

Cadenza is omitted. Reprinted from *Konzert für Cembalo (oder Klavier)*, edited by Christian Döbereiner (Frankfurt, 1927), pp. 3–19, 22. Reprinted by permission.

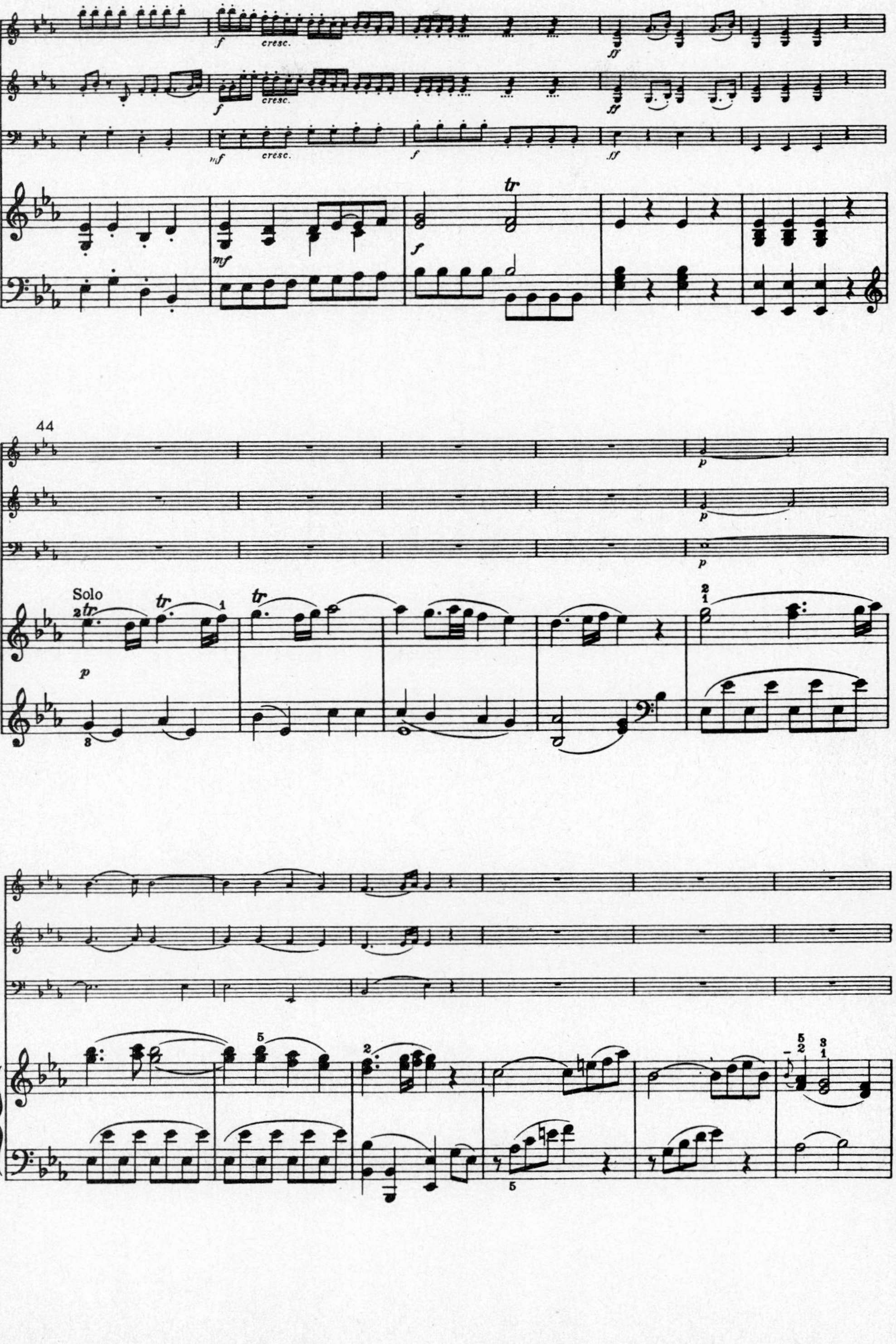
cresc.
44
Solo

Cadenza ad libitum

Wolfgang Amadeus Mozart (1756–91)
Piano Concerto in A Major, K. 488
(1786): Allegro (first movement)

Reprinted by permission of Bärenreiter-Verlag, Kassel, Basel, Tours, London from: *Neue Mozart Ausgabe*, Serie V, Werkgruppe 15, Band 7, edited by Hermann Beck (Kassel, 1959), pp. 3–34.

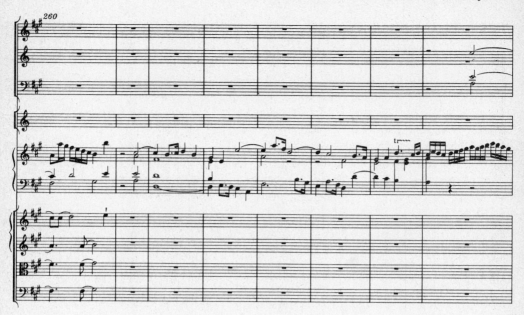

117

Giovanni Battista Pergolesi (1710–36)
Cantata [Orfeo] (1735)

a) *Recitative:* Nel chiuso centro

This recitative and aria open the cantata. Edited by Raimund Rüegge (Frankfurt, etc.: Henry Litolff's Verlag, © 1970), pp. 3–18. By permission.

don-na se-guen-do l'or-me per i-gnota vi - a, giun-se di Tra-cia, di Tra-cia il

va - te. Al suo do-lo - re qui sciol-se il fre - no, a rin-trac-ciar piè-

ta - te.   E qui nel mu-to or - ro - re,   in   dol-ci ac - cen - ti   all' al - me sven - tu -

ra - te   sul-la ce - tra nar - ran-do i suoi tor-men - ti,   tem-prò la pe - na   e de-bel-lò lo

sde-gno   del bar-ba-ro si -gnor   del cie-co re -gno.

b) *Aria:* Euridice, e dove, e dove sei?

di - ta   do-v'è il sol de gli oc - chi mie-i?   Chi fa-rà che tor - ni in vi -ta?   Chi al mio

cor la ren-de - rà

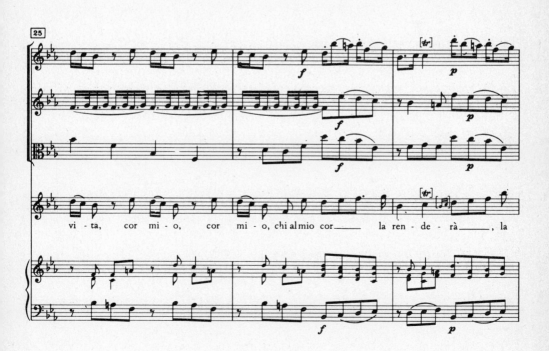

vi - ta, cor mi - o, cor mi - o, chi al mio cor ___ la ren - de - rà ___, la

ren - de - rà?   Ah,

do - ve, do-ve se-i Eu-ri - di -ce? E do-ve se - i? Chi m'a-scol-ta? Chi m'ad-

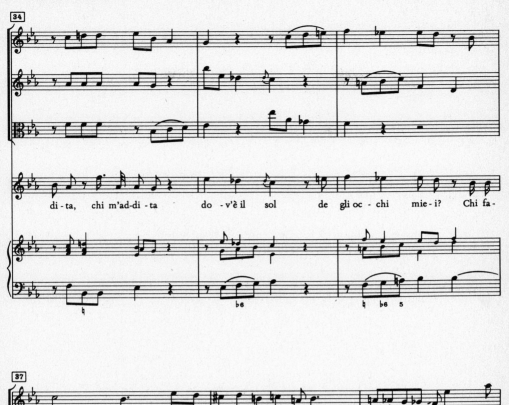

di - ta, chi m'ad-di - ta   do - v'è il sol   de gli oc - chi   mie - i?   Chi fa -

rà che tor-ni in vi - ta?   Chi al mio   cor la   ren-de - rà_____   ?chi al mi - o

cor_____ la ren - de - rà? Eu - ri - di - ce, do - ve se - i, e do - ve, do - ve

se - i? Cor mi - o, mia vi - ta, cor mi - o! Chi m'a-

scol-ta, chi m'ad-di-ta Eu-ri-di-ce? Do-v'è? Do-v'è? Chi al mio cor la

ren-de-rà? Chi al mio cor___ la ren-de-rà? la ren-de-

rà?

Pre - da fu d'in-giu-sta mor-te.   Io di-rò, se tra voi re -sta, tra voi re -sta

l'a - do-ra - ta mi - a con-sor-te, che pie - tà più non si de-sta, che giu-

sti - zia più non v'ha, no, no, non v'ha,   pie - tà,   giu - sti - zia più non

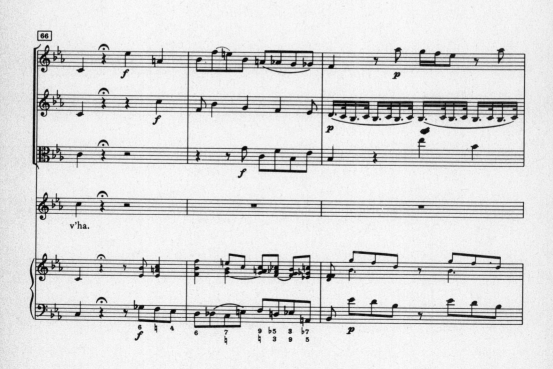

v'ha.

Dal segno ﹩ al Fine

Nel chiuso centro, ove ogni luce assonna,
All'or che pianse in compagnia d'amore,
Della smarrita donna
Seguendo l'orme per ignota via,
Giunse di Tracia il vate.
Al suo dolore qui sciolse il freno,
A rintracciar piètate.
E qui nel muto orrore,
In dolci accenti all'alme sventurate
Sulla cetra narrando i suoi tormenti,
Temprò la pena e debellò lo sdegno

Del barbaro signor del cieco regno.

Euridice, e dove, e dove sei?
Chi m'ascolta, chi m'addita?
Dov'è il sol de gli occhi miei?
Chi farà che torni in vita?
Chi al mio cor la renderà?
Mia vita, cor mio.
Preda fu d'ingiusta morte.
Io dirò, se tra voi resta,
L'adorata mia consorte,
Che pietà più non si desta,
Che giustizia più non v'ha.

Into that closed center, where all light sleeps,
accompanied by love, he wept,
for the woman who disappeared;
following her footprints along unknown paths,
the Thracian poet arrived.
To his sorrow he here gives free rein,
to arouse compassion.
And here in silent horror,
in sweet accents to the unhappy souls,
on the kithara narrating his torments,
he tempers the punishment and subdues
       the wrath
of the barbarous lord of the dark kingdom.

Euridice, where, o where are you?
Who will listen, who will help me?
Where is the sun of my eyes?
Who can make her return to life?
Who will return her to my heart?
My life, my heart.
Prey was she to an unjust death.
I must say, if among you she remains—
My adored bride—
then mercy does not stir in you,
then there is no longer any justice.

118

Jean-Jacques Rousseau (1712–78)
Le Devin du Village (1752): Scene 1, Air, *J'ai perdu tout mon bonheur*

Reprinted from *Le Devin du Village*, edited by Charles Chaix (Geneva: Édition Henn, c1924), pp. 11–17.

COLETTE

J'ai perdu tout mon bonheur,	I have lost all my happiness,
J'ai perdu mon serviteur.	I have lost my servant.
Colin me délaisse.	Colin forsakes me.
Hélas! il a pu changer!	Alas, he could have changed.
Je voudrais n'y plus songer.	I would rather stop dreaming about it.
J'y songe sans cesse.	Yet I dream about it incessantly.

(*Récit*).

Il m'aimait autrefois, et ce fut mon malheur . . .	He loved me once, and this was my bad luck . . .
Mais quelle est donc celle qu'il me préfère?	But who, then, is she whom he prefers?
Elle est donc bien charmante!	She must be very charming!
Imprudente bergère,	Imprudent shepherdess,
Ne crains tu point les maux	do you not fear at all the misfortunes
Que j'éprouve en ce jour?	that I am experiencing today?
Colin a pu changer; tu peux avoir ton tour . . .	Colin could have changed; you may have your turn . . .
Que me sert d'y rêver sans cesse?	What good does it do to dream about it incessantly.
Rien ne peut guérir mon amour	Nothing can cure my love
Et tout augmente ma tristesse.	and everything increases my sorrow.
J'ai perdu mon serviteur . . . etc.	I have lost all my happiness . . . etc.
Je veux le haïr; je le dois . . .	I want to hate him: I must do it . . .
Peut-être il m'aime encor . . .	Perhaps he loves me still . . .
Pourquoi me fuir sans cesse?	Why do I flee incessantly?
Il me cherchait tant autrefois.	He used to look for me once.
Le devin du canton fait ici sa demeure:	The soothsayer of the canton makes his home here.
Il sait tout; il saura le sort de mon amour.	He knows all; he will know the fate of my love.
Je le vois et je veux m'éclaircir en ce jour.	I see him, and I want this clarified today.

Libretto by the composer

119

Christoph Willibald Gluck (1714–87)
Orfeo ed Euridice (1762): Act II, Scene 1 (excerpt)

Ballo

Reprinted by permission of Bärenreiter-Verlag, Kassel, Basel, Tours, London from *Sämtliche Werke,* Abteilung I, Bd. I, edited by A. A. Abert and Ludwig Finscher (Kassel, 1963), pp. 55–75.

Coro

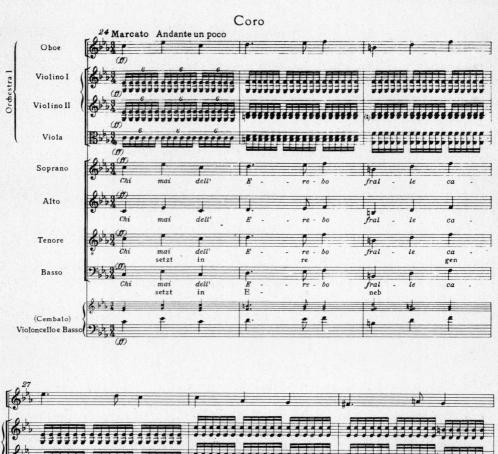

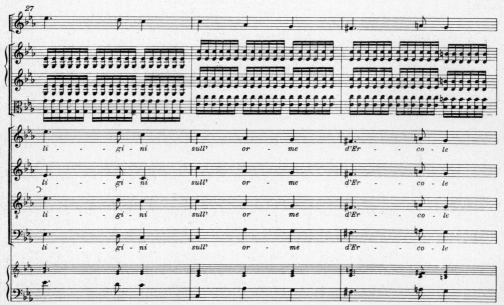

Ballo

Coro

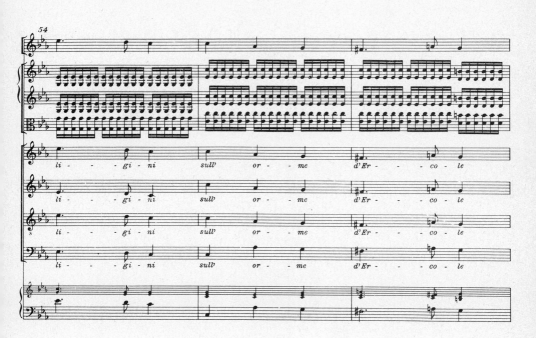

gliur - li   di   Cer - - be - ro,   se un   dio   non   è!

gliur - li   di   Cer - - be - ro,   se un   dio   non   è!

gliur - li   di   Cer - - be - ro,   se un   dio   non   è!

gliur - li   di   Cer - - be - ro,   se un   dio   non   è!

Segue il Ballo, girando intorno ad Orfeo per spaventarlo.

Ballo

Maestoso

Oboe I

Oboe II

Corno I,II in Mi♭/Es

Violino I

Violino II

Viola

(Cembalo)
Violoncello e Basso

lor, vi ren-da al-men pie - to - se il mio bar - ba-ro— do-lor!

Nò!

Nò!

Nò!

Nò!

bar - ba - ro   do - lor,   il__ mio   bar - - ba - ro   do - - lor!

CHORUS

Chi mai dell'Erebo	Who from Erebos
Fralle caligini	through the dark mists,
Sull'orme d'Ercole	in the footsteps of Hercules
E di Piritoo	and of Peirithous
Conduce il piè?	would ever set forth?
D'orror l'ingombrino	He would be blocked with horror
Le fiere Eumenidi,	by the fierce Eumenides
E lo spaventino	and frightened by
Gli urli di Cerbero,	the shrieks of Cerberus,
Se un dio non è.	unless he were a god.

ORPHEUS

Deh, placatevi con me.	Please, be gentle with me.
Furie, Larve, Ombre sdegnose!	Furies, specters, scornful phantoms!

CHORUS

No! . . . No! . . .	No! . . . No! . . .

ORPHEUS

Vi renda almen pietose	Let it at least make you merciful,
Il mio barbaro dolor!	my cruel pain!

Libretto by RANIERO DE' CALZABIGI

120

Wolfgang Amadeus Mozart
Don Giovanni, K. 527 *(1787)*; Act I, Scene 5

a) *No. 3, Aria:* Ah chi mi dice mai

Reprinted by permission of Bärenreiter-Verlag, Kassel, Basel, Tours, London from: *Neue Mozart Ausgabe*, Serie II, Werkgruppe 5, Bd. 17, edited by Wolfgang Plath and Wolfgang Rehm (Kassel, 1968), pp. 64–90.

*) Vorschlag zur eventuellen Auszierung der Fermate:

Recitative: Chi è là

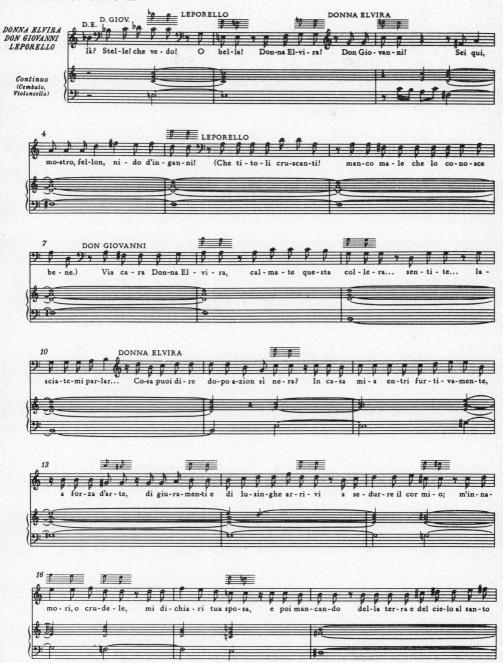

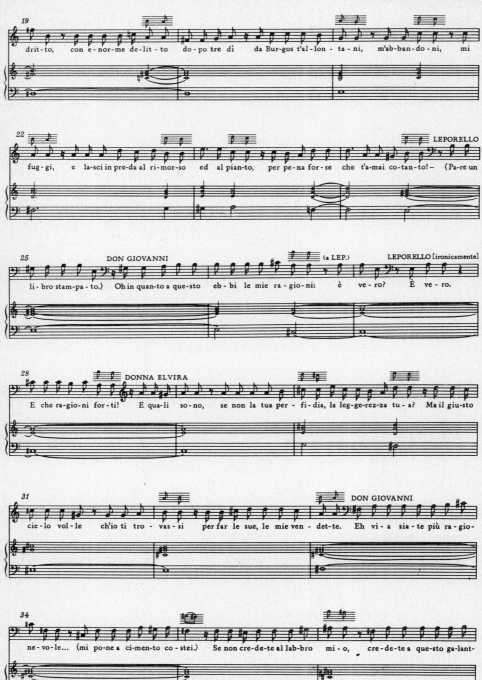

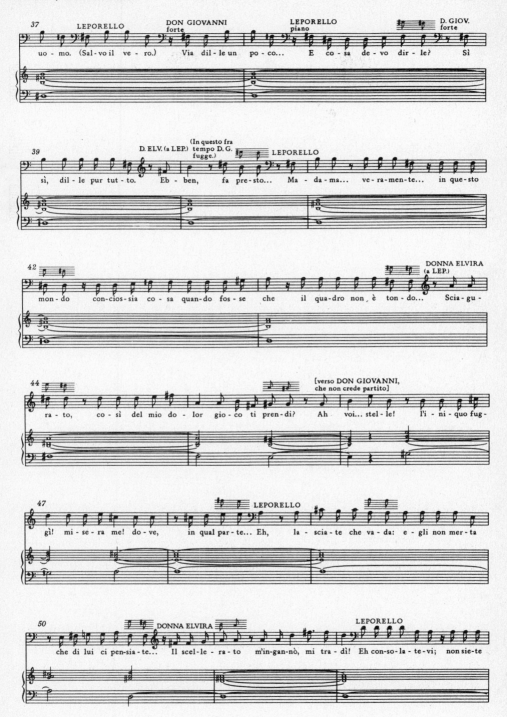

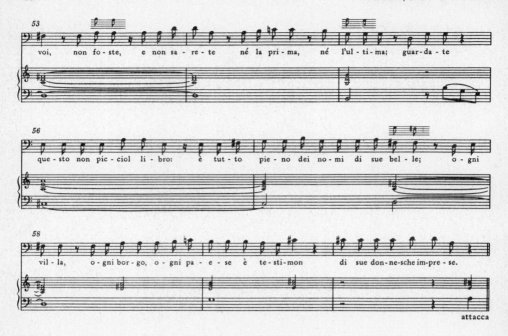

attacca

b) *No. 4, Aria:* Madamina! Il catalogo e questo

*) Vgl. Vorwort.

*) Vorschlag zur eventuellen Auszierung der Fermate:

*) Vorschlag zur eventuellen Auszierung der Fermate:

*) Zu einem im Autograph nach T. 153 gestrichenen Takt vgl. Krit. Bericht.

DONNA ELVIRA

Ah, chi mi dice mai,	Ah, who will ever tell me
Quel barbaro dov'è,	where that barbarian is,
Che per mio scorno amai,	whom, to my shame, I loved,
Che mi mancò di fè,	who failed to keep faith?
Ah, se ritrovo l'empio,	Ah, if I ever find the scoundrel,
E a me non torna ancor,	and to me he does not return,
Vo' farne orrendo scempio,	I shall brutally slaughter him.
Gli vo' cavare il cor.	I shall take out his heart.

DON GIOVANNI
(*to Leporello*)

Udisti? Qualche bella	Did you hear? Some beauty
Dal vago abbandonata.	by her lover abandoned.
Poverina! poverina!	Poor girl! Poor girl!
Cerchiam di consolare il suo tormento.	Let us try to console her torment.

LEPORELLO
(*aside*)

Così ne consolò mille e ottocento.	Thus he consoled a thousand and eight hundred.

DON GIOVANNI

Signorina! Signorina!	Signorina, Signorina!

DONNA ELVIRA

Chi è là?	Who goes there?

DON GIOVANNI

Stelle! che vedo!	Heavens! Whom do I see?

LEPORELLO
(*aside*)

O bella! Donna Elvira!	O this is nice! Donna Elvira!

DONNA ELVIRA

Don Giovanni!	Don Giovanni!
Sei quì, mostro, fellon, nido d'inganni!	You're here, monster! Felon, nest of deceits!

LEPORELLO
(*aside*)

Che titoli cruscanti!	Such Tuscan insults!
Manco male che lo conosce bene.	At least you know him well.

DON GIOVANNI

Via, cara Donna Elvira,	Now, dear Donna Elvira,
Calmate questa collera . . .	calm your anger . . .
Sentite . . . lasciatemi parlar.	Listen . . . let me speak.

DONNA ELVIRA

Cosa puoi dire, dopo azion sì nera?	What can you say, after such a black deed?
In casa mia entri furtivamente,	You entered my house furtively
A forza d'arte,	through trickery.

Di giuramenti e di lusinghe arrivi
A sedurre il cor mio:
M'innamori, o crudele,
Mi dichiari tua sposa,
E poi mancando della terra e del cielo
Al santo dritto,
Con enorme delitto
Dopo tre dì da Burgos t'allontani.
M'abbandoni, mi fuggi
E lasci in preda al rimorso ed al pianto,
Per pena forse che t'amai cotanto.

With oaths and flattery you succeded
in seducing my heart.
I fell in love.
You proclaimed me your bride,
and without earthly or heavenly writ
or legality,
with high crime, rather,
after three days you left Burgos.
You abandoned me; you fled
and left me a prey to remorse and to tears,
as penance, perhaps, for loving you so.

LEPORELLO
(*aside*)

Pare un libro stampato!

She sounds like a printed book.

DON GIOVANNI

Oh in quanto a questo, ebbi le mie ragioni!   As far as that's concerned, I had my reasons.

(*to Leporello*)

È vero.

It's true.

LEPORELLO

È vero, e che ragioni forti!

It's true, and what good reasons!

DONNA ELVIRA

E quali sono, se non per la tua perfidia,
La leggerezza tua?
Ma il giusto cielo volle ch'io ti trovassi,

Per far le sue, le mie vendette.

And what were they, if not your perfidy,
your trifling?
But the just heavens willed that I should find
  you
to have both its and my revenge.

DON GIOVANNI

Eh via, siate più ragionevole!
(Mi pone a cimento costei!)
Se non credete al labbro mio,
credete a questo galantuomo.

Now, now, be more reasonable.
(She pins me to the wall, this one.)
If you do not believe it from my lips,
believe this gentleman.

LEPORELLO

(Salvo il vero)

(Except for the truth.)

DON GIOVANNI
(*loudly*)

Via, dille un poco . . .

Go on, tell her something . . .

LEPORELLO
(*softly*)

E cosa devo dirle?

And what should I tell her?

DON GIOVANNI
(*loudly*)

Sì, sì, dille pur tutto.

Yes, yes, tell her everything.

DONNA ELVIRA

Ebben, fa presto . . .   Well, hurry up . . .

DON GIOVANNI
(*flees*)
LEPORELLO

Madama . . . veramente . . . in questo mondo   Madam . . . truthfully . . . in this world
Conciossia cosa quando fosse   notwithstanding that
Che il quadro non è tondo.   a square is not a circle.

DONNA ELVIRA

Sciagurato! così del mio dolor gioco ti prendi?   Scoundrel! thus of my anguish you jest?

(*to Don Giovanni, who, she thinks, has not left*)

Ah voi . . . stelle! l'iniquo fuggi!   Ah, you . . . heavens! You, the
                                                 guilty one, flees.
Misera me! dove? in qual parte . . .   Poor me! Where? In what direction?

LEPORELLO

Eh lasciate che vada; egli non merta   Let him go; he does not deserve
Che di lui ci pensiate.   that you should think of him.

DONNA ELVIRA

Il scellerato m'ingannò, mi tradì!   The rascal deceived me, he betrayed me.

LEPORELLO

Eh, consolatevi: non siete voi,   Oh, console yourself: you are not,
Non foste, e non sarete né la prima   were not the first, and will not be the last.
Né l'ultima: guardate questo non picciol libro; Look at this little book;
È tutto pieno dei nomi di sue belle;   it is full of the names of his conquests;
Ogni villa, ogni borgo, ogni paese   every village, every suburb, every country
È testimon di sue donnesche imprese.   is a testimony to his womanizing.

Madamina!   Madamina,
Il catalogo è questo   this is the catalog
Delle belle che amò il padron mio;   of the beauties that my lord loved;
Un catalogo egli è che ho fatt'io;   it is a catalog that I made myself.
Osservate, leggete con me!   Observe! Read with me.
In Italia seicento e quaranta,   In Italy, six hundred forty,
In Almagna due cento e trent'una,   in Germany two hundred thirty-one,
Cento in Francia, in Turchia novant'una,   a hundred in France, in Turkey ninety-one,
Ma in Ispagna son già mille e tre.   but in Spain there are a thousand and three.
V'han fra queste contadine,   Among these there are farm girls,
Cameriere, cittadine,   maids, city girls,
V'han contesse, baronesse,   there are countesses, baronesses
Marchesane, principesse,   marchionesses, princesses,
E v'han donne d'ogni grado,   and there are women of every rank,
D'ogni forma, d'ogni età.   every shape, and every age.
In Italia . . .   In Italy . . .
Nella bionda egli ha l'usanza   In a blonde he usually
Di lodar la gentilezza,   praises her gentility,
Nella bruna la costanza,   in a brunette her constancy,
Nella bianca la dolcezza;   in the white-haired, sweetness;

Vuol d'inverno la grassotta,   he wants, in winter, a plump one,
Vuol d'estate la magrotta;   he wants in summer a rather thin one;
E' la grande maestosa;   and the large one is majestic;
La piccina è ognor vezzosa.   the petite one is always charming.
Delle vecchie fa conquista   Of the old he makes a conquest
Pel piacer di porle in lista;   for the pleasure of adding them to the list;
Ma passion predominante   but his dominant passion
È la giovin principiante;   is the young beginner.
Non si picca se sia ricca,   He is not bothered if she is rich,
Se sia brutta, se sia bella,   if she's ugly, if she's pretty,
Purchè porti la gonnella: as long as she wears a skirt.
Voi sapete quel che fa.   You know what it is he does.

Libretto by LORENZO DA PONTE

This composition was first published in a longer version (96 measures) as a *Pastorale* in the *Second Divertimento for Piano with Accompaniment of a String Quartet* (Moscow, *ca.* 1811; London, *ca.* 1811–12). In 1815 it appeared in the present version as the first of three *Romances for Piano* (Leipzig, 1815), eventually becoming one of the *Nocturnes*, usually called No. 8, but actually No. 9 (see Cecil Hopkinson, *A Bibliographical Thematic Catalogue of the Works of John Field*, London, 1961, p. 33). Reprinted from *Nocturnes*, rev. by Louis Koehler (Frankfurt, etc., Peters n.d., pl. no. 6515), pp. 28–31.

122 Frédéric Chopin *(1810–49)*
Nocturne in E-flat Major, Opus 9, No. 2 *(1830–31)*

Reprinted from *Nocturnes*, rev. by Herrmann Scholtz (Frankfurt, etc., Peters, n.d., pl. no. 9025), p. 8–10.

123   Franz Liszt *(1811–86)*
Etudes d'exécution transcendante: No. 4, *Mazeppa*

The *Etudes d'exécution transcendante* were first published as *Etudes pour le piano en douze exercises* (Paris, 1827); they were revised as *Grandes Etudes* in 1837. The title "Mazeppa" dates from the 1852 edition. Reprinted by permission of Bärenreiter-Verlag, Kassel, Basel, Tours, London from: *Neue Ausgabe sämtlicher Werke,* Serie I, Vol. I (Kassel, 1970), pp. 15–28.

il canto espressivo ed appassionato assai

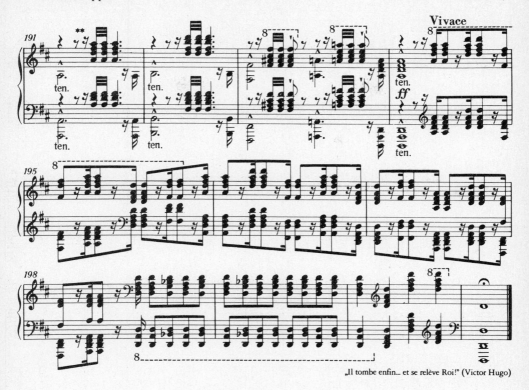

„Il tombe enfin... et se relève Roi!" (Victor Hugo)

124

Franz Liszt
Nuages gris (1881)

125

Hector Berlioz (1803–69)
Roméo et Juliette, Symphonie dramatique, Opus 17: Scherzo, *La Reine Mab, ou la Fée des songes*

First performance, 1839.

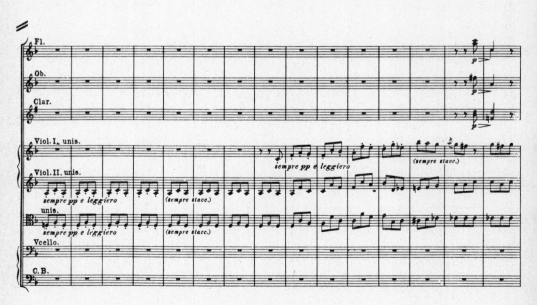

Allegretto. (♩=138.)

Deux fois plus lent que l'autre mouvement. Une mesure de ce ¾ doit donc équivaloir à trois mesures du ⅜ précédent.
Zweimal so langsam wie das vorhergehende Zeitmaass. Ein Takt dieses ¾ also gleichwerthig drei Takten des vorhergehenden ⅜.
Twice as slow as the previous tempo. A bar of this ¾ is therefore equal to 3 bars of the previous ⅜.

378

Allegretto. (♩=138.)

378

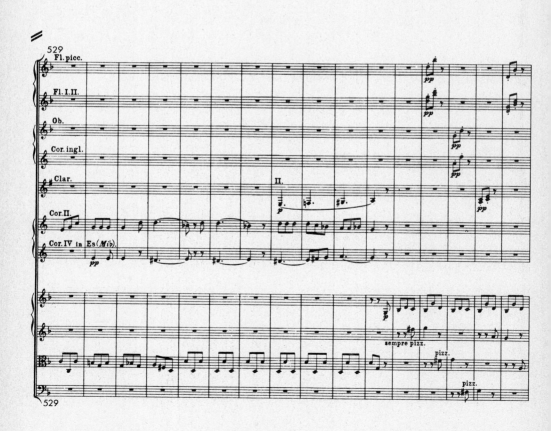

Coup frappé avec une baguette d'éponge sur une Cymb.ordinaire. Il faut tenir la Cymbale suspendue avec la main gauche et frapper avec la main droite.
Schlag mit einem Schwammschlägel auf ein gewöhnliches Becken. Das Becken muss frei aufgehängt in der linken Hand gehalten und mit der rechten
On ordinary cymbal struck with a sponge-headed drum-stick. The cymbal must be suspended free, held in the   [geschlagen werden.
left hand and struck with the right.

Cinelli. *f* **Laissez vibrer l'instrument!**
Das Instrument vibriren lassen.
The instrument to continue vibrating.

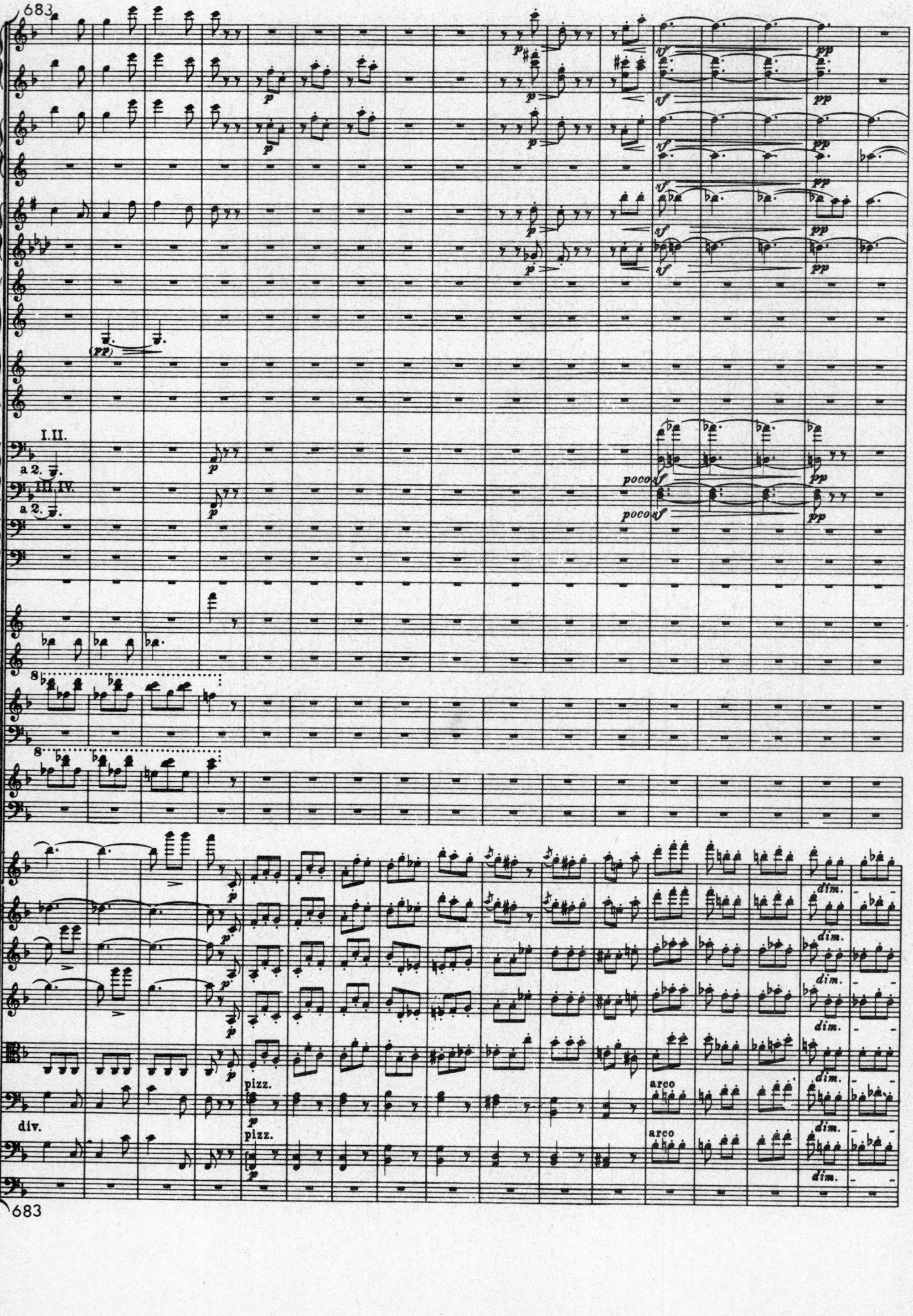
683
p
sf
pp
(pp)
I.II.
a 2.
III.IV.
a 2.
poco sf
8
pizz.
arco
div.
dim.
683

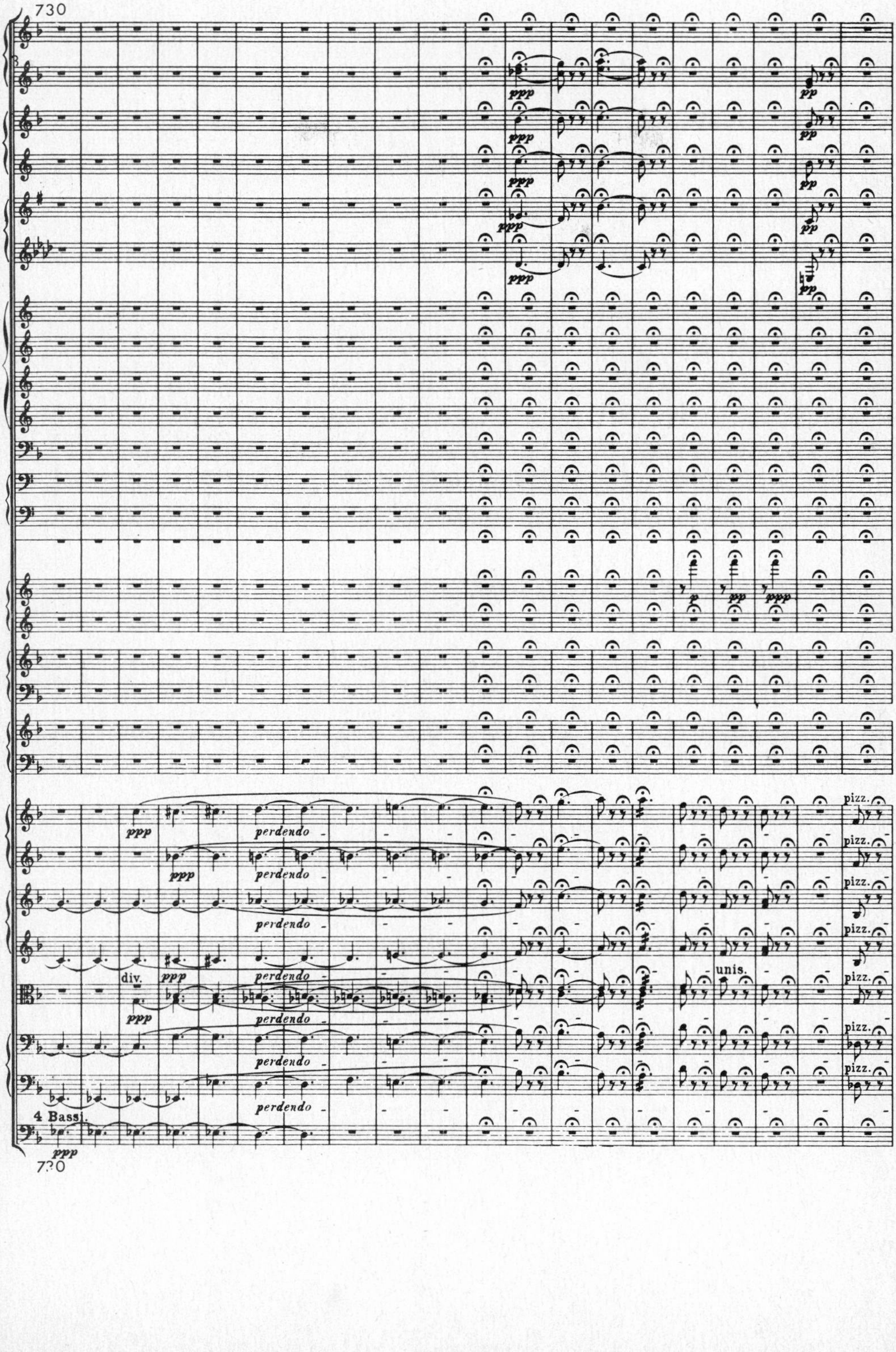
730
ppp
pp
ppp
perdendo
div.
unis.
pizz.
4 Bassi.
730

Fl.p. Presto.
Più animato. (♩. = 168.)
Fl. I.
Fl. II.
cresc.
a 2.
I. II.
III. IV.
Viol. I. unis.
Viol. II. unis.
arco
tenuto e perdendo
(sempre stacc.)
Presto.
Più animato. (♩. = 168.)

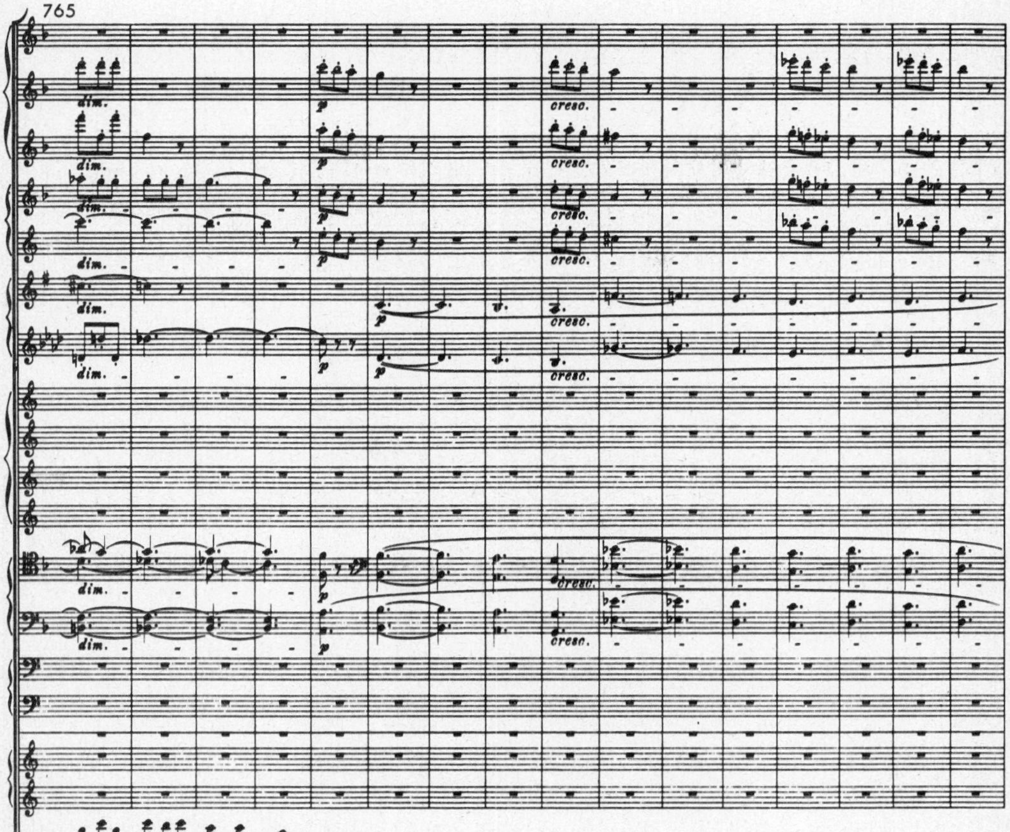
765
dim.
p
cresc.
765

Fl.picc.
Fl.I.II.
a 2.
in F (Fa).
II.
IV.
poco f
pizz.
div.
unis.
poco cresc.
cresc.
Tutti.
682

Felix Mendelssohn (1809–47)
Incidental Music to *A Midsummer's Night's Dream*, Opus 61 (*1843*): Scherzo

126

New York: Dover, 1975, pp. 55–71, reprinted from the Breitkopf & Härtel *Musik zu Sommernachtstraum von Shakespeare* (Leipzig, 1874–77).

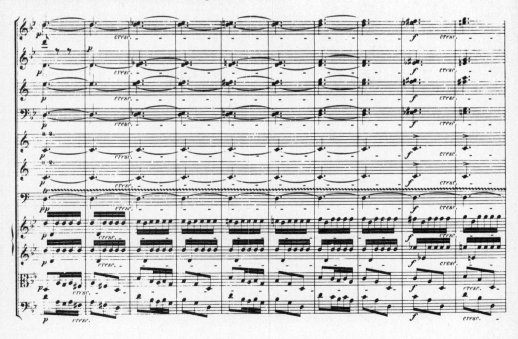

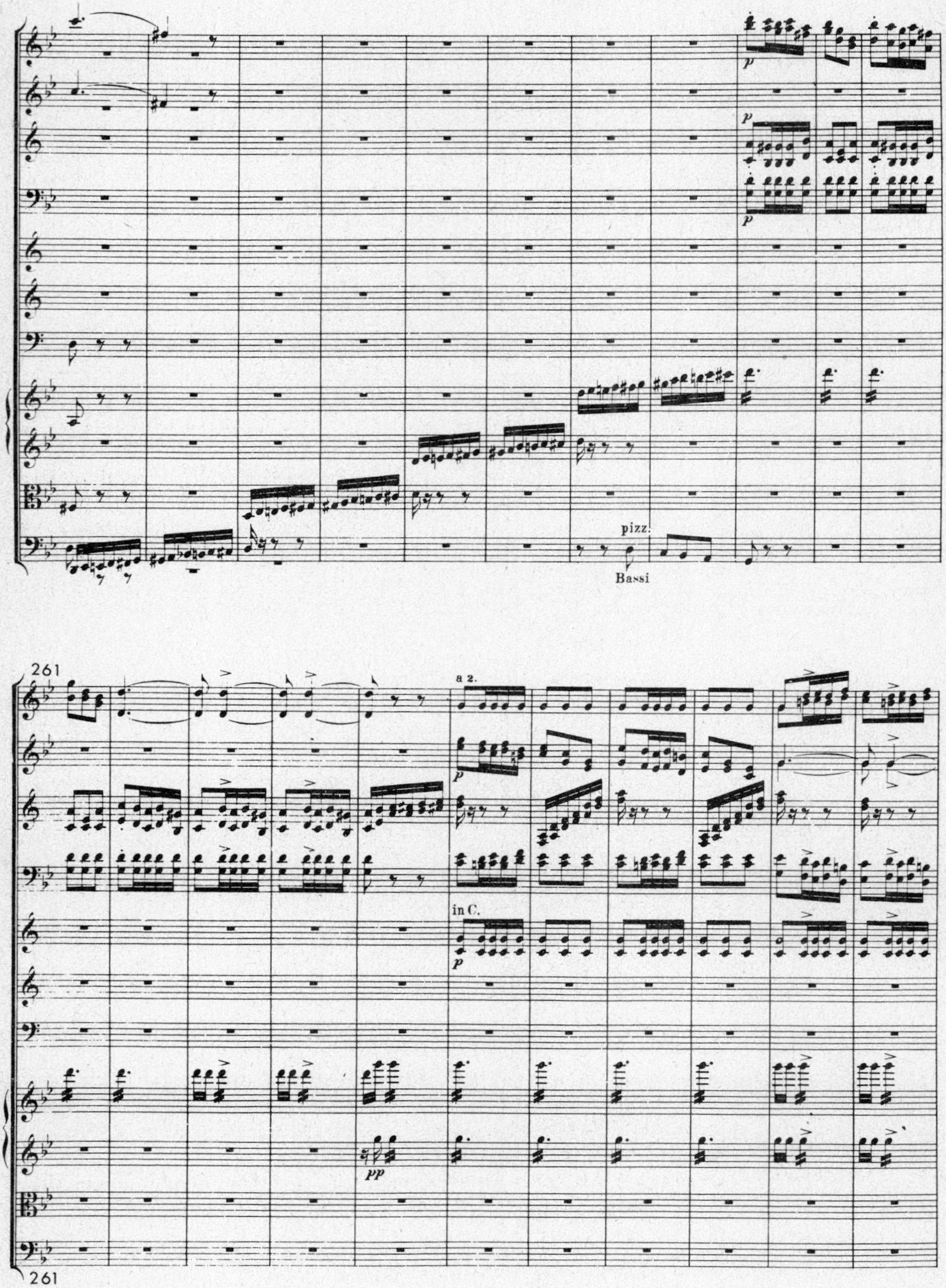
pizz.
Bassi
261
a 2.
in C.
p
pp
261

cresc.
dim.
dim.
dim.
dim.
pp
pp
pp
dim.
dim.
dim.
dim.

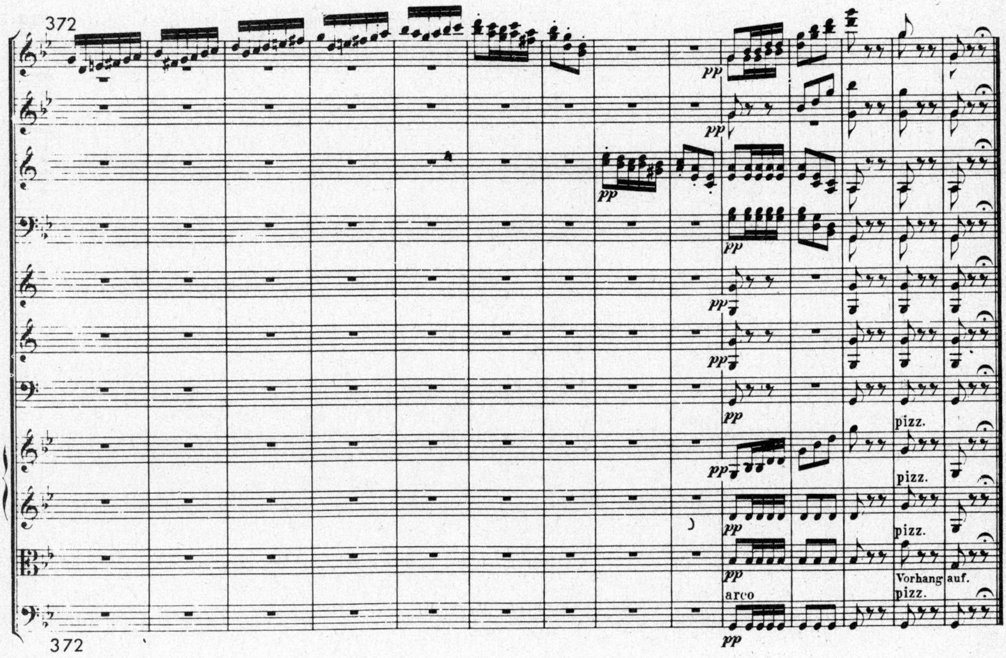
372
pp
pp
pp
pp
pp
pp
pp
pp
pp
pp
pizz.
pizz.
pizz.
Vorhang auf.
arco
pizz.
pp
372

127 Edward MacDowell (1861–1908)
Suite for Orchestra, Opus 48: Dirge-like, mournfully (fourth movement)

First performance, 1896. New York: Associated, n.d., pp. 73–79, reprinted from Breitkopf & Härtel (Leipzig, n.d.).

Johannes Brahms (1833–97)
Piano Quintet in F Minor, Opus 34
(1864): Scherzo

128

Reprinted from Editions Eulenberg, 1954, pp. 35–47.

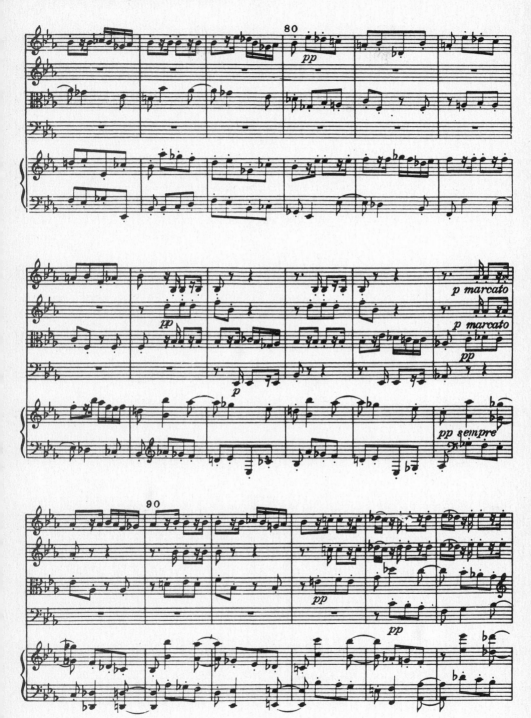

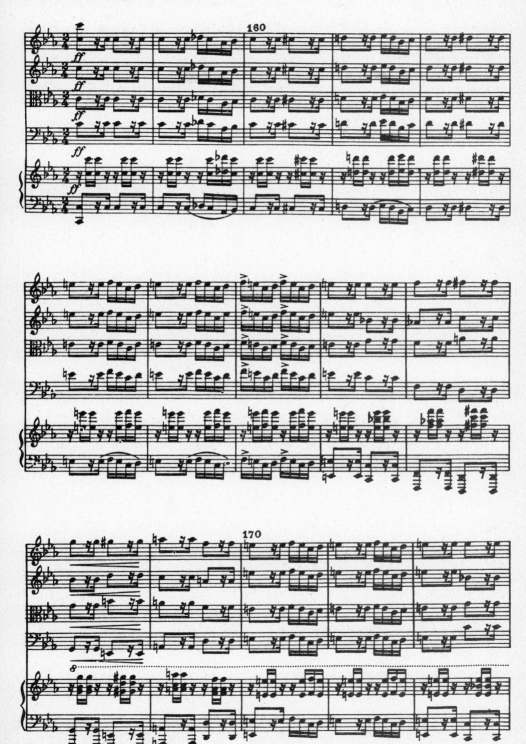

Scherzo da Capo sin al Fine

Franz Schubert *(1797–1828)*
Kennst du das Land (1815)

129

Compare this setting of Mignon's song from Goethe's *Wilhelm Meister* to Schumann's, p. 334 and Wolf 's, p. 339. *Franz Schubert Complete Works* Vol. 14 (New York, Dover, 1965), pp. 155–58, reprinted from the Breitkopf & Härtel critical edition (Leipzig, 1884–97).

Kennst du das Land, wo die Zitronen blühn,

Im dunkeln Laub die Gold-Orangen glühn,
Ein sanfter Wind vom blauen Himmel weht,
Die Myrte still und hoch der Lorbeer steht?
Kennst du es wohl? Dahin, dahin
Möcht' ich mit dir, o mein Geliebter, ziehn.

Kennst du das Haus? Auf Säulen ruht sein Dach,
Es glänzt der Saal, es schimmert das Gemach,
Und Marmorbilder Stehn und sehn mich an:

Was hat man dir, du armes Kind, getan?
Kennst du es wohl? Dahin, Dahin
Möcht' ich mit dir, o mein Beschützer, ziehn.

Kennst du den Berg und seinen Wolkensteg?
Das Maultier sucht im Nebel seinen Weg;

In Höhlen wohnt der Drachen alte Brut;

Es stürzt der Fels und über ihn die Flut.
Kennst du ihn wohl? Dahin! Dahin
Geht unser Weg! o Vater, lass uns ziehn!

Do you know the country where the lemon trees blossom?
Among dark leaves the golden oranges glow.
A gentle breeze from blue skies drifts.
The myrtle is still, and the laurel stands high.
Do you know it well? There, there
would I go with you, my beloved,

Do you know the house? On pillars rests its roof.
The great hall glistens, the room shines,
and the marble statues stand and look at me, asking:
"What have they done to you, poor child?"
Do you know it well? There, there
would I go with you, oh my protector,

Do you know the mountain and its path?
The muletier searches in the clouds for his way;
in the caves dwells the dragon of the old breed.
The cliff falls, and over it the flood.
Do you know it well? There, there
leads our way; oh father, let us go!

130

Robert Schumann *(1810–56)*
Kennst du das Land, Opus 79, No. 29
[Opus 98a, No. 1] *(1849)*

Compare this setting to Schubert's, p. 329 and Wolf's, p. 339. Reprinted from *Sämtliche Lieder* Vol. II, edited by Max Friedlaender (Frankfurt, 19—), pp. 212–15.

hin,   da - hingeht unser Weg, o Va - ter, laß uns ziehn!

For a translation of the text, see p. 333.

Hugo Wolf *(1860–1903)*
Kennst du das Land *(1888)*

131

Compare this setting to Schubert's, p. 329 and Schumann's, p. 334. Reprinted from *Ausgewählte Lieder*, edited by Elena Gerhardt (Frankfurt: Peters, 1932), pp. 134–41. By permission.

laß _ uns ziehn! _____

For a translation of the text, see p. 333.

132

Gustav Mahler (1860–1911)
Kindertotenlieder (1902): No. 1, Nun will die Sonn' so hell aufgehn

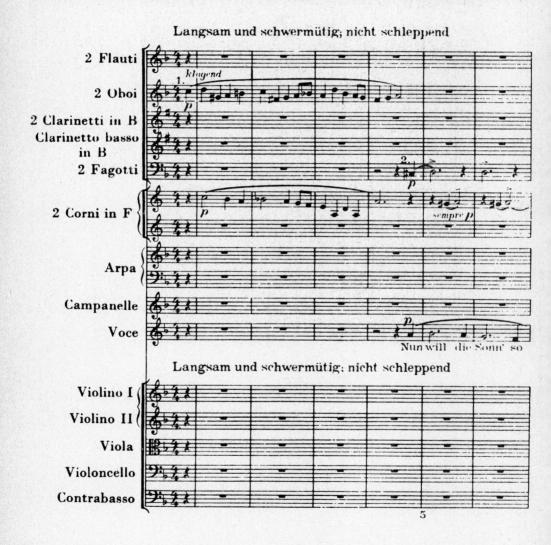

Reprinted from Edition Eulenburg, n.d., pp. 1–11.

Nun will die Sonn' so hell aufgehn,
Als sei kein Unglück die Nacht geschehn!
Das Unglück geschah nur mir allein!
Die Sonne, sie scheinet allgemein!

Du musst nicht die Nacht in dir verschränken,

Musst sie ins ew'ge Licht versenken!
Ein Lämplein verlosch in meinem Zelt!
Heil sei dem Freudenlicht der Welt.

FRIEDRICH RÜCKERT

Now will the sun so brightly rise again,
as if no misfortune occurred during the night.
The misfortune happened to me alone.
The sun shines for everyone.

You must not become tangled up with the
night in yourself.
You must be immersed in perennial light.
A little lamp went out in my tent.
Blessed be the joyous light of the world.

ROSINA

U na vo ce po co fa   qui nel cor   mi ri suo no;   il mio

First performance 20 February 1816. Reprinted from the piano-vocal score based on the critical edition of the orchestral
score (1969) (Milan, Ricordi n.d.), pp. 102–109. Reprinted by permission.

dol-ce, a-mo-ro-sa, mi la-scio reg-ge-re, mi la-scio

reg-ge-re, mi fo gui-dar, mi fo-gui-dar. Ma se mi

toc-ca-no dov'è il mio de-bo-le, sa-rò u-na vi-pe-ra, sa-

-rò, e cen-to trap-po-le pri-ma di ce-de-re fa-rò gio-

car, fa-rò gio-car, e cen-to trap-po-le pri-ma di

ROSINA

Una voce poco fa
Qui nel cor mi risuonò.
Il mio cor ferito è già,
E Lindor fu che il piagò.
Sì, Lindoro mio sarà,
Lo giurai la vincerò
Il tutor ricuserò,
Io l'ingegno aguzzerò.
Alla fin s'accheterà,
E contenta io resterò.
Sì, Lindoro mio sarà . . .

Io sono docile, son rispettosa,
Sono obbediente, dolce amorosa,
Mi lascio reggere, mi fo guidar.
Ma se mi toccano dov'è il mio debole,
Sarò una vipera, e cento trappole
Prima di cedere farò giocar!

A voice a short while ago
here in my heart resounded.
My heart is already wounded,
and Lindoro is the culprit.
Yes, Lindoro will be mine.
I swore that I would win.
The guardian I shall refuse.
I shall sharpen my wits.
In the end he will be appeased,
and I shall be happy.
Yes, Lindoro will be mine . . .

I am docile, I am respectful,
I am obedient, sweetly loving;
I let myself be governed, to be led.
But if they touch my weaker side,
I can be a viper, and a hundred tricks,
I'll play before I give in!

Libretto by CESARE STERBINI
after BEAUMARCHAIS

Vincenzo Bellini (1801–35)
Norma: Act I, Scene 4, Scena e Cavatina, *Casta Diva*

134

First performance 26 December 1831. Reprinted from *Norma* (Milan, Ricordi 1974), pp. 61–84. Reprinted by permission.

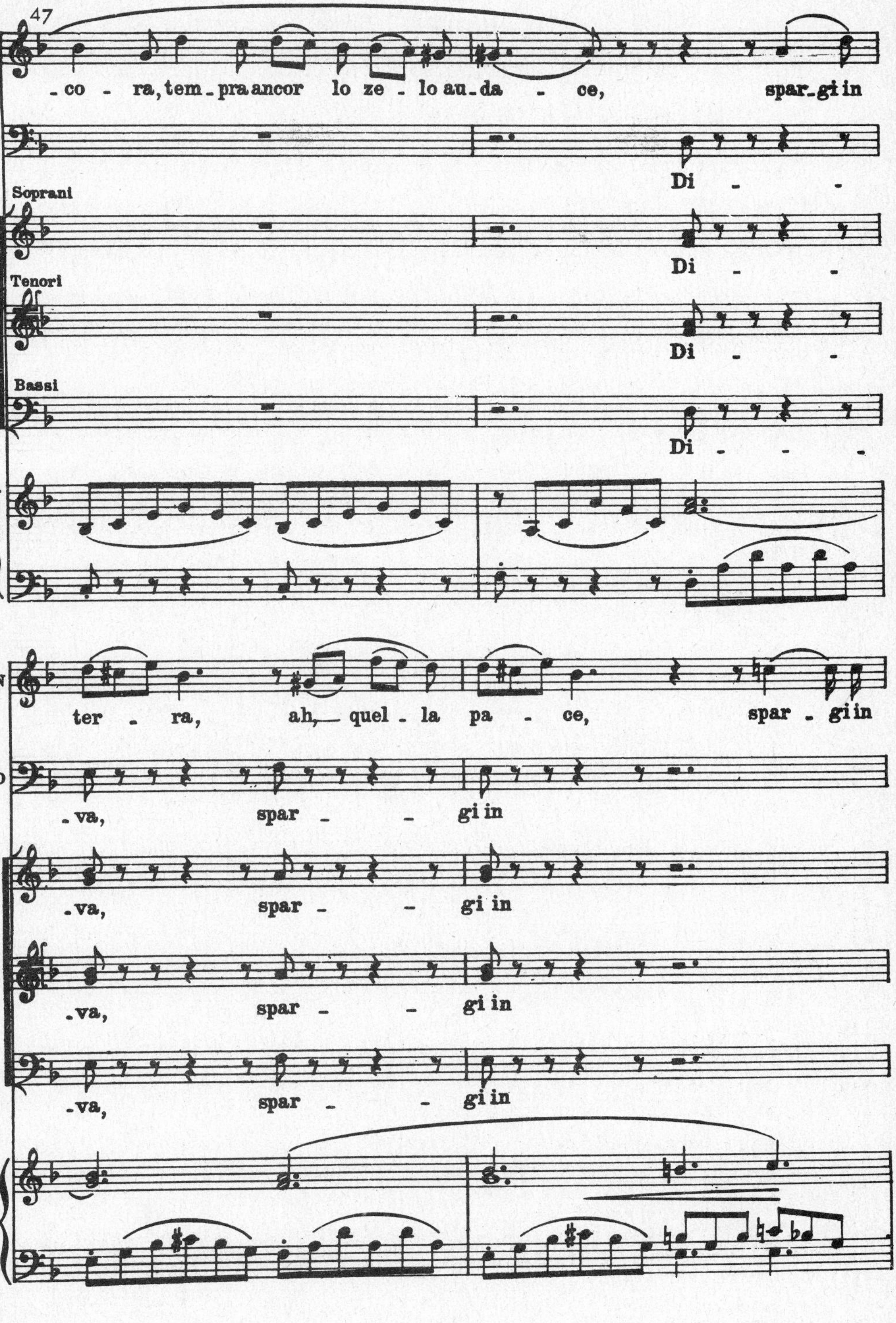
47
N
-co - ra, tem-pra ancor lo ze - lo au-da - ce, spar-gi in
O
Di - -
Soprani
Di - -
Tenori
Di - -
Bassi
Di - - -
CORO
N
ter - ra, ah, quel - la pa - ce, spar - gi in
O
-va, spar - - gi in
-va, spar - - gi in
-va, spar - - gi in
-va, spar - - gi in

fo _ sco   chiegga il san _ gue   dei Ro _ ma _ ni,   dal dru _

_ i _ di _ co   de _ lu _ bro __ la mia __ vo ___ ce

tuo __ ne _ rà.

OROVESO

Tuo _ ni;   e un sol del po _ pol

Soprani

Tuo _ ni;   e un sol __ del __ po _ pol __

Tenori

Tuo _ ni;   e un sol __ del __ po _ pol

Bassi

Tuo _ ni;   e un sol del po _ pol

con forza

rag - gio tuo __ se - re - no; e vi _ ta __ nel tuo

Opp.

se - no e pa - - - - -

con abbandono

se - no e pa - - - - - - tria e cie - lo a -

pp

Opp.

- vrò, _____ e

126

- vrò, _____ e cie - - - - - lo a -

bel _ lo a me ri _ tor _ na del fi _ do a _ mor pri _

_mie _ ro, e con _ tro il mon _ do in _ tie _ ro_____ di _

_fe _ sa a_____ te sa _ rò. Ah!____

bel _ lo a me_____ ri tor_____ na del____

NORMA

Casta Diva, che inargenti	Chaste Goddess, who plates with silver
Queste sacre antiche piante,	these sacred ancient plants,
A noi volgi il bel sembiante;	turn your lovely face towards us,
Senza nube e senza vel!	unclouded and unveiled.
Tempra, o Diva, tu de' cori ardenti,	Temper, o, Goddess, these ardent hearts,
Tempra ancora lo zelo audace,	o temper their bold zeal.
Spargi in terra, ah, quella pace,	Spread over the earth that peace
Che regnar tu fai nel ciel.	that you make reign in heaven.
Fine al rito; e il sacro bosco	The rites are finished, and the sacred wood,
Sia disgombro dai profani.	be it cleared of intruders.
Quando il Nume irato e fosco,	When the angry and gloomy god
Chiegga il sangue dei Romani,	demands the blood of the Romans,
Dal Druidico delubro	from the Druidic shrine
La mia voce tuonerà.	my voice will resound.

TUTTI

Tuoni; e un sol del popol empio	Let it be heard, and let not a single one of the impious race
Non isfugga al giusto scempio;	escape our just massacre,
E primier da noi percosso	and the first to feel our blows,
Il Proconsole cadrà,	the Proconsul will fall.

NORMA

Cadrà . . . punirlo io posso . . .	He will fall . . . punish him I can . . .
(Ma punirlo il cor non sa.)	(But to punish him my heart does not know how.)
(Ah! bello a me ritorna	(Ah, return to me, love,
Del fido amor primiero:	my faithful first love,
E contro il mondo intiero	and, against the entire world
Difesa a te sarò.	I shall be your defense.
Ah! bello a me ritorna	Ah, return to me, love,
Del raggio tuo sereno;	the serene radiance of your gaze;
E vita nel tuo seno	and living in your bosom
E patria e cielo avrò).	both homeland and heaven I'll possess).

CHORUS

Sei lento, si, sei lento,	How it drags on, sluggishly,
O giorno di vendetta;	this day of revenge;
Ma irato il Dio t'affretta	but the angry God hurries you
Che il Tebro condannò.	whom the Tiber condemned.

NORMA

(Ah! bello) . . .	(Ah, return) . . .

CHORUS

Sei lento . . .	How it drags . . .

NORMA

(Ah! riedi ancora	(Ah, return again
Qual eri allora	to what you were then
Quando, ah, quando il cor	when, oh, when my heart
Ti diedi allora).	I gave to you).

Libretto by FELICE ROMANI

First performance 29 February 1836. The division into scenes, not found in the score, is taken from Scribe's libretto.
Reprinted from *Les Huguenots* (Paris: Ph. Maquet & Cie., n.d.), pp. 172–210.

MARGUERITE

Oui, d'un heu-reux hymen pré-pa-ré ____ par mes soins J'ai dé-si_

dulce

_ré, Mes_sieurs, que vous fussiez té _ moins.

(La reine présente Raoul aux comtes de Saint-Bris et de Nevers, qui lui tendent la main.)

Sop.

Hon_neur, hon_neur à la plus bel _ le, honneur! Hà_

Tén.

Hon_neur, hon_neur à la plus bel _ le, honneur! Hà_

Basses

Hon_neur, hon_neur à la plus bel _ le, honneur! Hà_

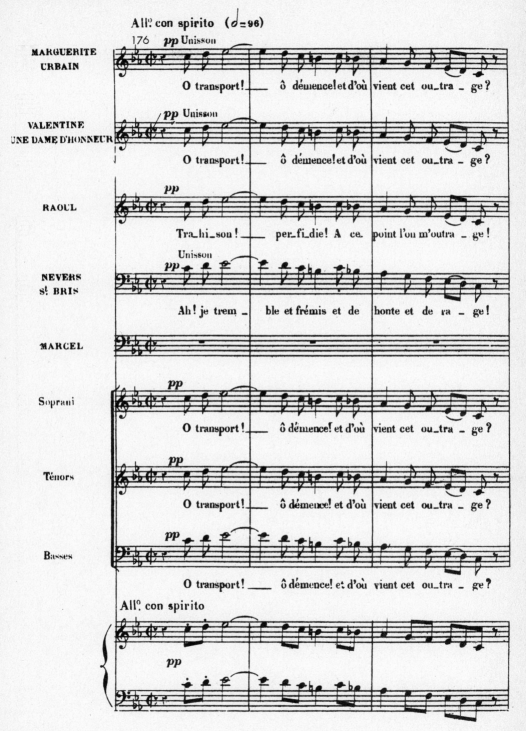

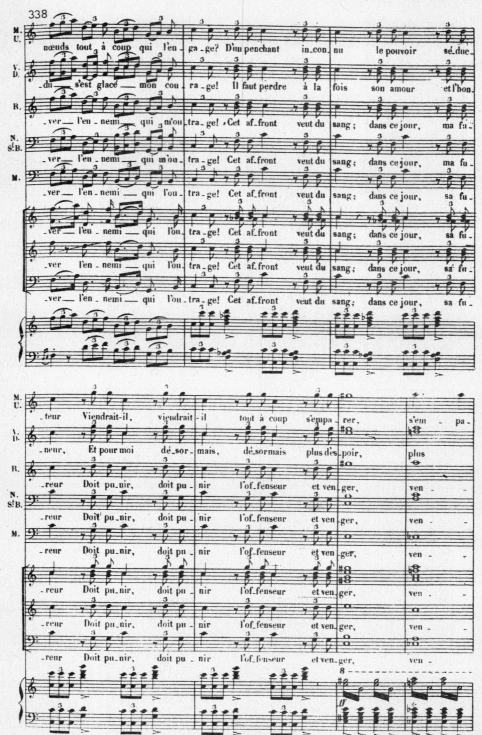

(St. Bris et Nevers entraînent Valentine à moitié évanouie, et sortent en défiant Raoul, qui veut les suivre et que retiennent les soldats de la reine.)

(The gentlemen of the court, led by St.–Bris and Nevers, enter during the ritornello
The Catholics are arranged on one side, the Protestants on the other).

MARGUERITE

Oui, d'un heureux hymen préparé par mes soins	Yes, of a happy marriage arranged with my blessing
J'ai désiré, Messieurs, que vous fussiez témoins.	I wished, Sirs, that you be the witnesses.

(The queen presents Raoul to the Counts of St.–Bris and Nevers, who extend their hands to him).

CHORUS

Honneur, honneur à la plus belle!	Honor, honor to her who is most beautiful!
Hâtons–nous d'accourir;	Let us hasten to approach.
C'est voler au plaisir!	Let us hurry to pleasure.

MARCEL
(arriving, all excited, taking Raoul aside)

Ah' qu'est–ce que j'apprends!	Ah, what do I hear?

(Raoul makes a sign to him to keep quiet).
(Marcel speaks softly to Raoul, but with indignation).

Vous avez recherché la main d'une Madianite!	You sought the hand of a Madianite?

RAOUL

Tais–toi!	Be quiet!

MARCEL

Sa maison est celle du péché.	Her house is a den of sin.

RAOUL

Tais–toi!	Be quiet!

MARGUERITE
(to St.–Bris and to Nevers, after having read some papers that a courier has delivered)

Mon frère Charles IX, qui connait votre zèle.	My brother, Charles IX, who knows your ardor,
Tous les deux, à Paris, dès ce soir vous rappelle,	summons you both to Paris for this evening,
Pour un vaste projet que j'ignore.	for a great plan that I know nothing about.

NEVERS, ST.–Bris

A sa loi	To his commands
Nous nous soumettons.	we submit.

MARGUERITE

Oui, mais d'abord à la mienne:	Yes, but first of all to mine.
Grâce à cet hymen, abjurant toute haine,	Thanks to this marriage that renounces all hate,
Prononcez donc tous trois, comme aux pieds de l'autel,	pronounce, all three, as if at the foot of the altar,
D'une éternelle paix, prononcez le serment solennel!	of eternal peace, pronounce a solemn oath.

(to the Protestant gentlemen and to the Catholics)

Et vous aussi, messieurs, qu'un seul voeu vous enchaîne!

And you, too, gentlemen, may a single vow bind you together.

(All surround the Queen to swear the oath).

RAOUL, ST.–BRIS, NEVERS

Par l'honneur, par le nom que portaient mes ancêtres,
Nous jurons,
Par le roi, par ce fer à mon bras confié,
Ah! jurons.

By our honor, by the name that our ancestors bore,
we swear;
by the King, by this sword on my arm,
ah, let us swear.

ALL

Nous jurons!

We swear.

RAOUL, ST.–BRIS, NEVERS

Devant vous nous jurons éternelle amitié.

In your presence we swear eternal friendship.

MARCEL
(aside)

Par Luther, par la foi que je tiens de mes maîtres,
Ah! jurons,
Par la croix, par ce fer à mon bras confié,

By Luther, by the faith that I have from my masters,
ah, we swear,
by the cross, by this sword on my arm,

ALL

Ah! jurons,
Guerre à mort, Rome, à toi tes soldats et tes prêtres,
Oui, jurons!
Et jamais entre nous amitié, ni pitié!

Ah, we swear.
War to death, Rome, to you, your soldiers and your priests,
yes, let us swear.
And let there never be between us friendship nor mercy!

ALL, EXCEPT MARCEL

Par l'honneur, par le nom que portaient mes ancêtres,
Par le Dieu qui punit tous les traîtres,
Nous jurons devant vous, éternelle amitié!

By our honor, by the name my ancestors bore,
by the god who punishes all the traitors,
we swear in your presence eternal friendship.

RAOUL, NEVERS, ST.–BRIS

Providence, mère tendre,
Sur la terre fais descendre
La concorde, pour nous rendre,
Tous des frères, tous amis.

Providence, tender mother
make descend to the earth
harmony, to make us
all brothers, all friends.

MARCEL

Providence, mère tendre
Sur mon maître, fais descendre
Ta lumière, pour le rendre
A ses frères, à tes fils!
Juste ciel!

Providence, tender mother,
on my Lord, make descend
your light, to return him
to his brothers, to your sons!
Just heavens!

MARGUERITE

Que le ciel daigne entendre et bénir, à jamais ces serments.

May heaven deign to hear and bless these oaths.

RÉCITATIF

Et maintenant je dois offrir à votre vue	And now I must offer to your sight
Votre charmante prétendue,	your charming fiancée,
Qui rendra vos serments faciles à tenir!	who will make your oath easy to keep.
(St.–Bris reappears, leading Valentine toward Raoul).	

RAOUL
(with muffled voice)

Ah! grand Dieu! qu'ai – je vu?	Ah! Great God! What do I see?

MARGUERITE

Qu'avez–vous?	What's wrong with you?

RAOUL
(barely able to speak)

Quoi! . . . c'est elle!	What! . . . It is she! She
Que m'offraient en ce jour . . .	whom they offer to me today.

MARGUERITE

Et l'hymen et l'amour!	Marriage and love, together!

RAOUL

Trahison! Perfidie!	Treason! Treachery!
Moi, son époux? jamais! jamais!	I, her spouse? Never! Never!

ALL

Ciel!	Heavens!

MARQUERITE, URBAIN, VALENTINE, A LADY OF HONOR

O transport! ô démence! et d'où vient cet out-rage?	O rapture! O madness! Whence comes this outrage?
A briser de tels noeuds quel délire l'engage?	To break these knots, what delirium inspires him?

RAOUL

A ce point l'on m'outrage!	At this point I am outraged!
Je repousse à jamais un honteux mariage!	I reject forever this shameful marriage!

NEVERS, ST.–BRIS

Ah! je tremble et frémis et de honte et de rage!	Ah I shake and shiver from shame and anger.
C'est à moi d'immoler l'ennemi qui m'ou-trage!	It is up to me to sacrifice the enemy who insults me!

MARCEL

Oui, mon coeur applaudit, cher Raoul, ton courage!	Yes, my heart applauds, dear Raoul, your courage!

CHORUS

Et pourqoui rompre ainsi le serment qui l'engage?	And why break thus the oath that he swore?

MARGUERITE, URBAIN, VALENTINE, A LADY OF HONOR

D'un penchant inconnu le pouvoir seducteur	Has an unknown impulse, its seductive power,
Viendrait-il tout à coup s'emparer de son coeur?	all of a sudden taken possession of his heart?

RAOUL

Plus d'hymen, je l'ai dit; et, fidèle à l'hon- No marriage, as I said. Loyal to my honor,
neur,
Je me ris désormais de leurs cris de fureur! I laugh now at their cries of fury.

NEVERS, ST.–BRIS

C'est son sang qu'il me faut pour calmer ma It is his blood that I need to calm my fury.
fureur,
Pour punir cet affront, pour venger mon hon- To punish this affront, to avenge my honor!
neur!

MARCEL

Chevalier et chrétien, écoutant seul l'honneur, Knight and Christian, listening only to his
conscience,
Il se rit désormais de leurs cris de fureur! he laughs now at their cries of fury.

CHORUS

Cet affront veut du sang; dans ce jour, sa This affront calls for blood. On this day his
fureur fury
Doit punir l'offenseur et venger son honneur! must punish the offender and avenge his
honor.

VALENTINE
(with pained expression)

Et comment ai–je donc mérité tant d'outrage? How did I deserve such an insult?
Dans mon coeur éperdu s'est glacé mon In my desolate heart has frozen my courage.
courage!

RAOUL

O douleur! triste sort! O misery! Sad destiny!
A ce point l'on m'outrage! To such a point they insult me!

NEVERS AND ST.–BRIS

Frémissant et tremblant, Shuddering and trembling,
Plein de honte et de rage, . . . full of shame and anger, . . .

MARCEL
(aside, in an outpouring of joy)

Seigneur, rempart et seul soutien du faible qui Lord, rampart and only support of the feeble
t'adore! who adore you!

MARGUERITE

Un semblable refus . . . Such a refusal . . .

RAOUL

N'est que trop légitime! Is only right!

MARGUERITE

Dites–m'en la raison. Give me a reason

RAOUL

Je ne le puis sans crime; I cannot without incriminating myself;
mais cet hymen, jamais! but this marriage, never!

MARGUERITE

O transport! ô démence! et pourquoi cet ou-   O rapture, o madness! And why this outrage?
trage?
A briser de tels noeuds quel délire l'engage?   To undo these knots what delirium inspires
                                                 him?

NEVERS AND ST.-BRIS
(*to Raoul*)

Sortons! Qu'il tombe sous nos coups!   Let's go. Let him fall beneath our blows.

RAOUL

D'un tel honneur mon coeur est plus jaloux!   Of such an honor my heart is too eager.

MARGUERITE

Arrêtez! Devant moi quelle insulte nouvelle!   Halt! In my presence, what new insult?
(*signaling an officer to disarm Raoul*)
Vous, Raoul, votre épée!   You, Raoul, your sword.
(*to St.–Bris*)
Et vous, oubliez-vous   And you, do you forget
Qu'à l'instant près de lui votre roi vous rap-   that at this moment your king summons you to
pelle?   his side?

RAOUL

Je les suivrai!   I shall follow them.

MARGUERITE

Non pas; près de moi dans ces lieux   No. Near me in this place
Vous restez!   you will remain.

ST.–BRIS

Le lâche est trop heureux   The coward is too happy
Que cette main royale ait un tel privilège!   that this royal hand have such a privilege.
C'est en vain qu'on pretend enchaîner mon   It's in vain that they claim they can enchain
courage;   my courage.

RAOUL
(*in a muffled voice, to St.–Bris*)

C'est vous qu'elle protège en désarmant mon   It is you she protects in disarming my hand,
bras,
Et bientôt je serai près de vous!   and soon I shall be close to you.

MARGUERITE

Téméraires! Tous les deux redoutez ma colère!   Fools! Both of you better dread my anger.

NEVERS AND ST.–BRIS

Je saurai retrouver l'ennemi, l'offenseur!   I shall know how to find the enemy, the of-
                                                 fender.

MARCEL

Oui! mon coeur applaudit Raoul de son noble   Yes, my heart applauds Raoul for his noble
courage!   courage.

CHORUS

C'est en vain qu'on prétend enchaîner son courage;	It's in vain that they claim they can enchain his courage.
Il saura retrouver l'ennemi qui l'outrage!	He will know how to find the enemy that offends.
Ah! partons, éloignons—nous!	Ah, let's go, let's get away.
Allons, partons, éloignons—nous!	Let's go, let's leave, let's get away.
Rien ne pourra sauver Raoul!	Nothing can save Raoul.

MARCEL
(aside, joyfully)

Tu nous défends encor, mon Dieu!	You defend us still, my God!

(*St.–Bris and Nevers drag Valentine, half fainting, and exit, defying Raoul, who wants to follow but is restrained by the Queen's soldiers*).

Libretto by EUGÈNE SCRIBE

<table>
<tr><td>

136

</td><td>

Carl Maria von Weber *(1786–1826)*
Der Freischütz

</td></tr>
</table>

a) *Overture*

First performance 18 June 1821. Reprinted by permission from *Der Freischütz* (Leipzig: C. F. Peters, n.d.), pp. 3–18, 56–59, and 93–99.

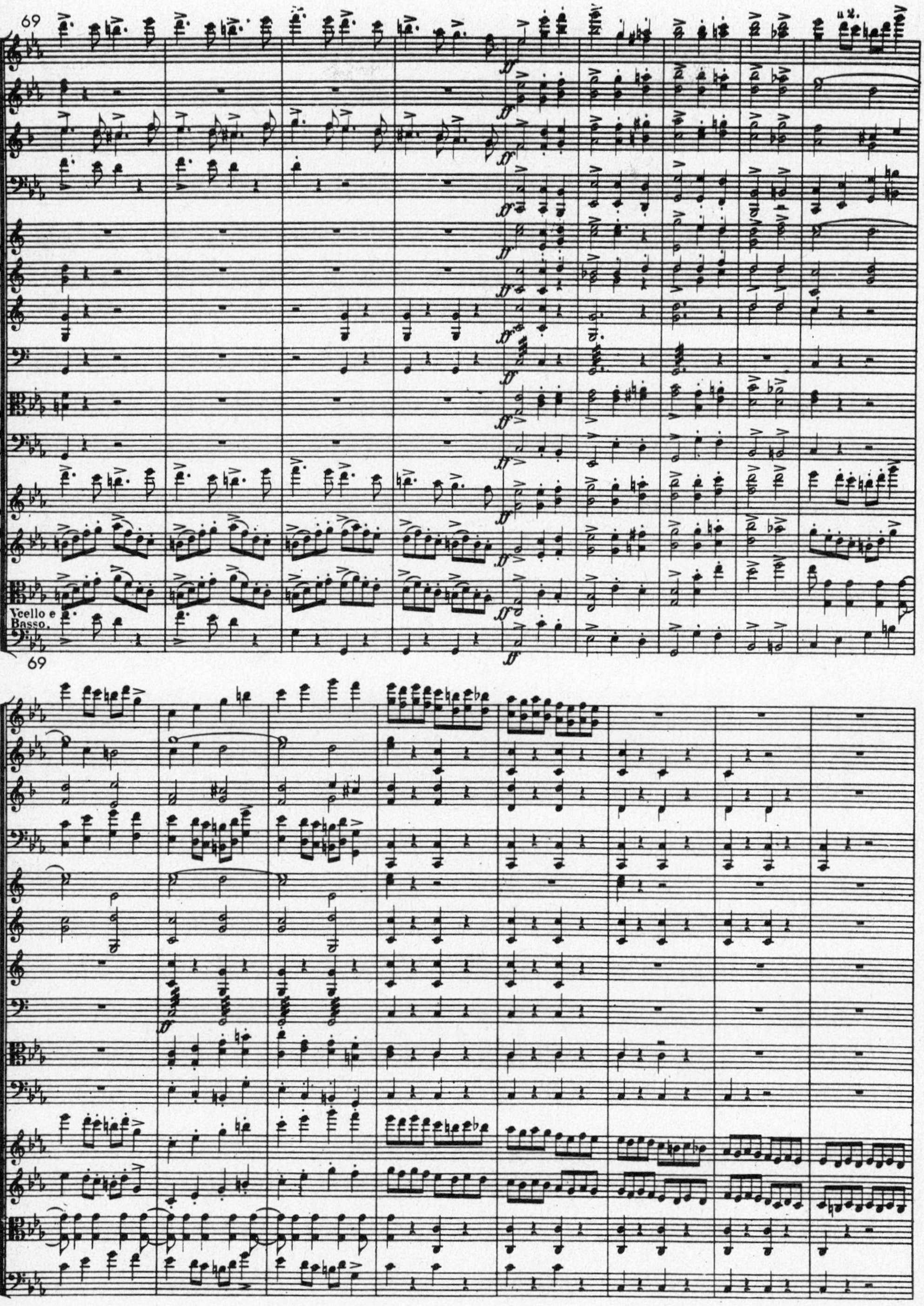
69
Vcello e Basso.
69

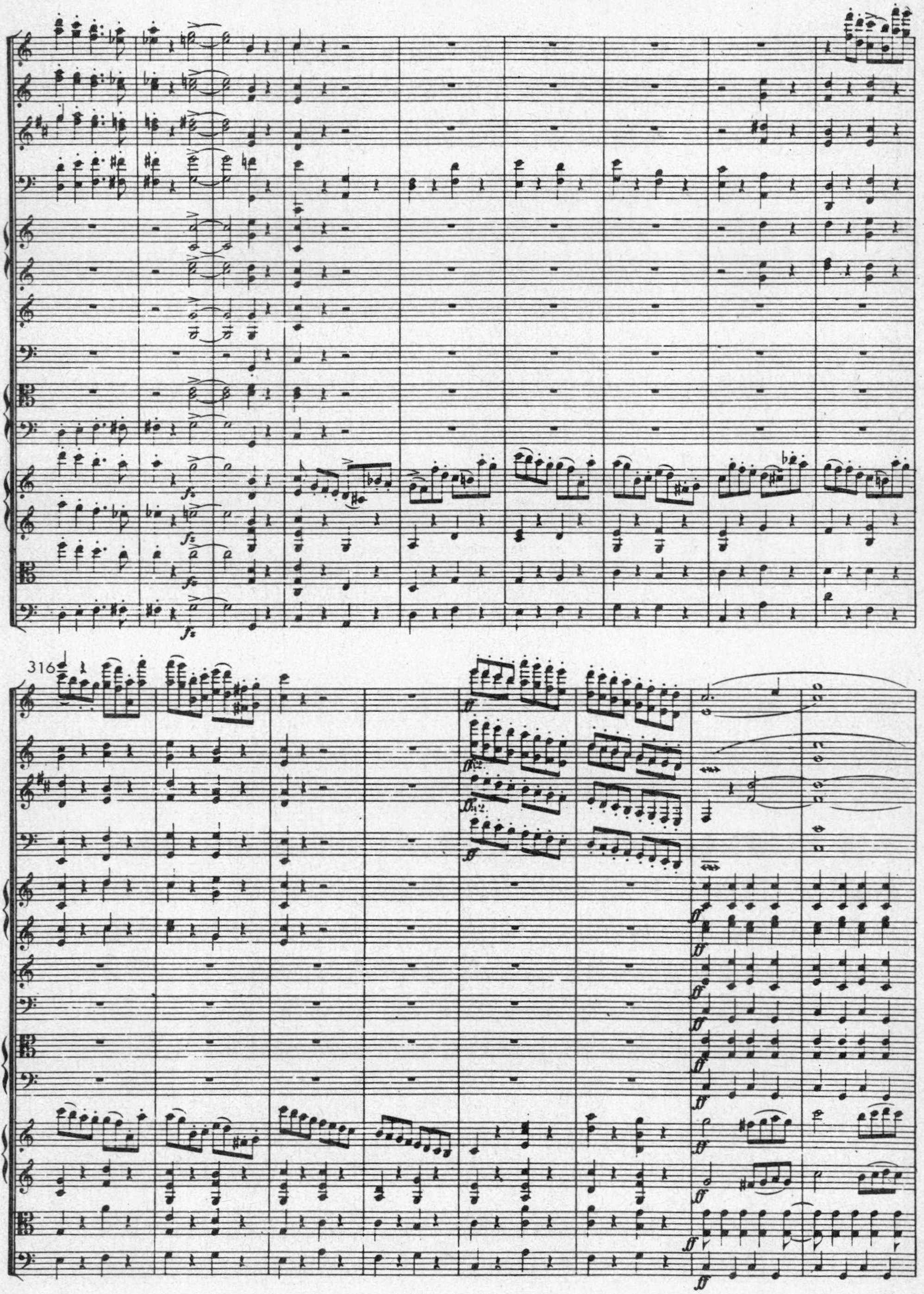
316

b) *Act I, Scene 3: Max's Aria,* Doch mich umgarnen finstre Mächte

458

c) *Act II, Scene 2: Agatha's Aria,*
   All' meine Pulse schlagen

All' meine Pulse schlagen und das Herz wallt unge - stüm.

Pfand der Hoffnung an.— Him — mel,— nimm des— Dan — kes Zäh — ren für — dies

53

Pfand — der Hoff — nung an! All' meine Pulse schlagen und das Herz wallt un — ge — stüm;

zückt ent - ge - gen ihm!

(*Samiel in the background with big strides moves slowly across the stage so that he is already on the opposite side by the outcry*)

MAX

Doch mich umgarnen finstre Mächte;
Mich fasst Verzweiflung, foltert Spott!
O, dringt kein Strahl durch diese Nächte?
Herrscht blind das Schicksal?
    Lebt kein Gott?

Thus sinister powers ensnare me.
Nearly to despair am I tormented, mocked.
Not a ray of light pierces through this night?
Does fate rule blindly?
    Is there no God?

AGATHA

All' meine Pulse schlagen,
Und das Herz wallt ungestüm.
Süss entzückt entgegen ihm!
Konnt' ich das zu hoffen wagen?
Ja, es wandte sich das Glück
Zu dem theuern Freund zurück,
Will sich morgen treu bewähren!
Ist's nicht Täuschung, ist's nicht Wahn?
Himmel, nimm des Dankes Zähren
Für dies Pfand der Hoffnung an.

All my pulses are beating,
and my heart throbs wildly.
Sweetly drawn am I to him.
Dare I hope for that?
Yes, there is a change of fortune,
for it returns to my dear friend.
Will it tomorrow prove to be true.
Is it not a deception; is it not an illusion?
Heaven, accept a grateful tear
as a guarantee for this hope.

       Libretto by FRIEDRICH KIND

Composed 1857–59; first performance 10 June 1865. Reprinted from *Tristan und Isolde,* edited by Felix Mottl (Frankfurt: Peters, 1914), pp. 85–102. Reprinted by permission.

SAILORS
(outside)

Auf das Tau!	Haul the line.
Anker ab!	Drop the anchor.

TRISTAN
(starting wildly)

Los den Anker!	Drop the anchor.
Das Steuer dem Strom!	Stern to the current.
Den Winden Segel und Mast!	Sail and mast to the wind.

(He takes the cup from Isolde)

Wohl kenn' ich Irlands	Well know I Ireland's
Königin,	Queen,
Und ihrer Künste	and her art's
Wunderkraft:	magic.
Den Balsam nützt' ich,	The balsam I used
Den sie bot:	that she brought.
Den Becher nehm' ich nun,	The goblet I now take
Dass ganz ich heut' genese.	so that I might altogether today recover.
Und achte auch	And heed also
Des Sünne eid's,	the oath of atonement,
Den ich zum Dank dir sage.	which I thankfully made to you.
Tristans Ehre,	Tristan's honor,
Höchste Treu!	highest truth.
Tristans Elend,	Tristan's anguish,
Kühnster Trotz!	brave defiance.
Trug des Herzens!	Betrayel of the heart,
Traum der Ahnung:	dream of presentiment,
Ew'ger Trauer	eternal sorrow,
Einz'ger Trost:	unique solace,
Vergessens güt'ger Trank,	forgetting's kindly draught,
Dich trink' ich sonder Wank.	I drink without wavering.

(He sits and drinks)
ISOLDE

Betrug auch hier?	Betrayed even in this?
Mein die Hälfte!	The half is mine!

(She wrests the cup from his hand,)

Verräter! Ich trink' sie dir!	Traitor, I drink to you!

(She drinks, and then throws away the cup. Both, seized with shuddering, gaze at each other with deepest agitation, still with stiff demeanor, as the expression of defiance of death fades into a glow of passion. Trembling grips them. They convulsively clutch their hearts and pass their hands over their brows. Then they seek each other with their eyes, sink into confusion, and once more turn with renewed longing toward each other).

ISOLDE
(with wavering voice)

Tristan!	Tristan!

TRISTAN
(overwhelmed)

Isolde!	Isolde!

ISOLDE
(*sinking on his chest*)

Treuloser Holder!   Treacherous lover!

TRISTAN

Seligste Frau!   Divine woman!
(*He embraces her with ardor. They remain in silent embrace*).

ALL THE MEN
(*outside*)

Heil! Heil!   Hail! Hail!
König Marke!   King Mark!
König Marke, Heil!   King Mark, hail!

BRANGÄNE
(*who, with averted face, full of confusion and horror, had leaned over the side, turns to see the pair sunk into a love embrace, and hurls herself, wringing her hands, into the foreground*).

Wehe! Weh!   Woe's me! Woe's me!
Unabwendbar   Inevitable,
Ew'ge Not   endless distress,
Für kurzen Tod!   instead of quick death!
Tör'ger Treue   Misleading truth,
Trugvolles Werk   deceitful work
Blüht nun jammernd empor!   now blossoms pitifully upward.
(*They break from their embrace*).

TRISTAN
(*bewildered*)

Was träumte mir   What did I dream
Von Tristans Ehre?   of Tristan's honor?

ISOLDE

Was träumte mir   What did I dream
Von Isoldes Schmach?   of Isolde's disgrace?

TRISTAN

Du mir verloren?   Are you lost to me?

ISOLDE

Du mich verstossen?   Have you repulsed me?

TRISTAN

Trügenden Zaubers Tückische List!   False magic's nasty trick!

ISOLDE

Törigen Zürnes Eitles Dräu'n!   Foolish wrath's vain menace!

TRISTAN

Isolde! Süsseste Maid!   Isolde, sweetest maiden!

ISOLDE

Tristan! Trautester Mann!   Tristan, most beloved man!

BOTH

Wie sich die Herzen wogend erheben,	How, heaving, our hearts are uplifted!
Wie alle Sinne wonnig erbeben!	How all our senses blissfully quiver!.
Sehnender Minne	Longing, passion,
Schwellendes Blühen,	swelling, blooms,
Schmachtender Liebe	languishing love,
Seliges Glühen!	blessed glow!
Jach in der Brust	Precipitate in the breast
Jauchzende Lust!	exulting desire!
Isolde! Tristan!	Isolde! Tristan!
Tristan! Isolde!	Tristan!. Isolde!
Welten entronnen	Escaped from the world,
Du mir gewonnen!	you have won me.
Du mir einzig bewusst,	You, my only thought,
Höchste Liebeslust!	highest love's desire!

(The curtains are now drawn wide apart. The entire ship is filled with knights and sailors, who joyfully signal the shore from aboard. Nearby is seen a cliff crowned by a castle. Tristan and Isolde remain lost in mutual contemplation, unaware of what is taking place).

BRANGÄNE
(to the women, who at her bidding ascend from below)

Schnell den Mantel,	Quick, the cloak,
Den Königsschmuck!	the royal robe.

(rushing between Tristan and Isolde)

Unsel'ge! Auf!	Up, unfortunate pair! Up!
Hört, wo wir sind.	See where we are!

(She puts the royal cloak on Isolde, who does not notice anything).

ALL THE MEN:

Heil! Heil!	Hail, hail!
König Marke!	King Mark!
König Marke, Heil!	King Mark, hail!

KURWENAL
(advancing cheerfully)

Heil Tristan!	Hail, Tristan!
Glücklicher Held!	Fortunate hero!
Mit reichem Hofgesinde	With splendid courtiers
Dort auf Nachen	there in the skiff
Naht Herr Marke.	Mark approaches.
Heil! wie die Fahrt ihn freut,	Ah, how the ride delights him,
Dass er die Braut sich freit!	for soon he will be wooing the bride.

TRISTAN
(looking up, bewildered)

Wer naht?	Who comes?

KURWENAL

Der König!	The King.

TRISTAN

Welcher König?	Which King?

(Kurwenal points over the side. Tristan stares stupefied at the shore).

ALL THE MEN
(*waving their hats*)

Heil! König Marke!   Hail, King Mark!

ISOLDE
(*confused*)

Marke! Was will er?   Mark! What does he want?
Was ist, Brangäne!   What is that, Brangäne?
Welcher Ruf?   What is the shouting?

BRANGÄNE

Isolde! Herrin!   Isolde! Mistress,
Fassung nur heut!   get hold of yourself.

ISOLDE

Wo bin ich? Leb' ich?   Where am I? Am I alive?
Ha! Welcher Trank?   Oh, what drink was it?

BRANGÄNE
(*despairingly*)

Der Liebestrank!   The love potion.

ISOLDE
(*stares, frightened, at Tristan*)

Tristan!   Tristan!

TRISTAN

Isolde!   Isolde!

ISOLDE
(*She falls, fainting, upon his chest*).

Muss ich leben?   Must I live?

BRANGÄNE
(*to the women*)

Helft der Herrin!   Help your mistress!

TRISTAN

O Wonne voller Tücke!   O rapture full of cunning!
O Truggeweihtes Glücke!   O fraudulently won good fortune!

ALL THE MEN
(*in a general acclamation*)

Heil dem König   Hail the King!
Kornwall, Heil!   Hail, Cornwall!

(*People have climbed over the ship's side, others have extended a bridge, and the atmosphere is one of expectation of the arrival of those that have been awaited, as the curtain falls*).

Giuseppe Verdi (1813–1901)
Il Trovatore: Part 4, Scene 1, No. 12: Scene, Aria, and Miserere

138

SCENA I. Si avanzano due persone ammantellate: sono Leonora e Ruiz.

RUIZ (sommessamente)

Siam giunti: ec-co la tor-re, o-ve di Stato ge-mono i pri-gio-nieri... Ah! l'infe-li-ce i-vi fu tratto!

LEO.

Vanne... lasciami; nè ti-mor di me ti

First performance 19 January 1853. Reprinted from *Il Trovatore*, edited by Mario Parenti (Milan: Ricordi, 1944), pp. 184–201. Reprinted by permission.

prenda. Salvarlo io potrò, forse.
Timor di

me?.. Sicu_ra, presta è la mia di _ fe _ sa!

In quest'oscura notte ravvolta, presso a te son i_o, e tu nol sai!.. Gemente

au_ra, che intorno spiri, deh, pi_e_to_sa, deh,__ pie_

_to _ sa gliar_re_cai miei so_spi_ri!

L. _ba _ scia, che tut _ ta m'in _ ve _ ste, al labbro il respi _ ro, i pal _ pi _ ti al

L. cor, il re _ spi _ ro, i pal _ pi _ ti al

L. cor!

MAN. (dalla torre)
Ah!............ che la mor _ te o _ gno _ ra è .... tar _ da nel ve _

Arpa

(*A wing in the palace of Aliaferia. At one end a window barred with iron. A very dark night.*
Two persons advance, wrapped in cloaks. They are Ruiz and Leonora).

RUIZ
(*softly*)

Siam giunti:	We have arrived:
Ecco la torre, ove di Stato	here is the tower, where the State's
Gemono i prigionieri! . . . Ah!	prisoners moan . . . Ah,
l'infelice	unhappy fate,
Ivi fu trattò!	it was here he was brought!

LEONORA

Vanne.   Go.
Lasciami, nè timor di me ti prenda.   Leave me alone, and don't worry about me.
Salvarlo io potrò forse.   Perhaps I'll be able to save him.

(Ruiz goes off).

Timor di me? . . . Sicura,   Fear for me? . . . Surely,
Presta è la mia difesa!   quick is my defense.

(Her eyes fasten on a jewel that ornaments her right hand).

In quest'oscura notte ravvolta,   Enveloped in this dark night,
Presso a te son io, e tu nol sai!   I am near to you, but you do not know it.
  Gemente   Moaning
Aura, che intorno spiri,   breeze that spirals around us,
Deh, pietosa gli arreca i miei sospiri!   o, for pity's sake, yield to my sighs!
D'amor sull'ali rosee   On the rose-colored wings of love,
Vanne, sospir dolente,   go, sad sigh,
Del prigioniero misero   the wretched prisoner's
Conforta l'egra mente . . .   sick soul to comfort . . .
Com'aura di speranza   Like a breeze of hope
Aleggia ın quella stanza: flap to that dungeon,
La desta alle memorie,   there to stir those memories,
Ai sogni dell'amor!   arouse dreams of love.
Ma, deh! non dirgli, improvvido,   But, please, tell him not, thoughtlessly,
Le pene del mio cor!   of the troubles of my heart.

LEONORA, MANRICO, & CHORUS

Miserere, d'un alma già vicina   Have mercy for a soul already near
Alla partenza che non ha ritorno.   to the departure that has no return.
Miserere di lei, bontà divina,.   Have mercy on him, Divine Goodness,
Preda non sia dell'infernal soggiorno.   that his soul not be victim of infernal sojourn.

LEONORA

Quel suon, quelle preci,   That sound, those prayers,
Solenni, funeste,   solemn, dismal,
Empiron quell'aere   that tune—they are replete
Di cupo terror!   with somber horror.
Contende l'ambascia,   Relieve the agony
Che tutta m'investe,   that overwhelms me,
Al labbro il respiro,   that robs my lips of breath,
I palpiti al cor!   that makes my heart palpitate.

MANRICO

Ah che la morte ognora   Ah, how death is ever
È tarda nel venir,   slow to arrive
A chi desia morir!   to him who desires to die!
Addio, Leonora, addio!   Farewell, Leonora, farewell!

LEONORA

Oh ciel! Sento mancarmi!   O heavens! I feel faint.

CHORUS

Miserere, etc.   Have mercy, etc.

LEONORA

Sull'orrida torre, ahi! par che la morte   Over that horrible tower, alas, it appears that death

Con ali di tenebre librando si va!   with its dark wings hovers.
Ah! forse dischiuse gli fian queste porte   Ah, perhaps the doors swing open to death
Sol quando cadaver già freddo sarà!   only when a cadaver is already cold.

MANRICO

Sconto col sangue mio   I expiate with my blood
L'amor che posi in te!   the love that I vowed to you.
Non ti scordar di me!   Forget me not.
Leonora, addio!   Leonora, farewell.

LEONORA

Di te, di te scordarmi!   I shall not forget you.
    Libretto by SALVATORE CAMMARANO

139 Anton Bruckner (1824–96)
Virga Jesse (Motet)

Composed 1885. Reprinted from *Virga Jesse* (New York: Peters, 1961). Reprinted by permission.

Virga Jesse floruit:
Virgo Deum et hominem genuit:
pacem Deus reddidit,
in se reconcilians ima summis.

Alleluja.

The rod of Jesse blossomed:
a virgin brought forth God and man;
peace God restored,
in himself reconciling the lowest with the
      highest.

Alleluia.

Claude Debussy (1862–1918)
Trois Nocturnes (1893/4): Nuages

140

See p. 679. Mussorgsky *Les jours de fête*, for the source of the figure in the clarinets and bassoons. Reprinted from *Nocturnes* (New York: Kalmus, n.d.), pp. 2–18.

32

37

42

46

50

59

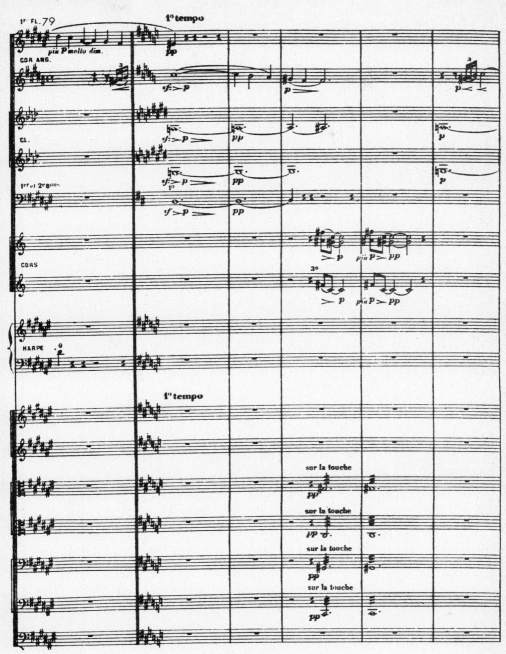

141

Maurice Ravel *(1875–1937)*
Le Tombeau de Couperin (1917):
Menuet

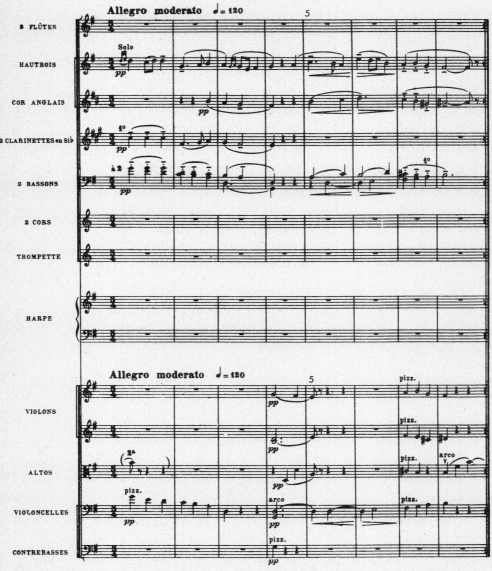

Orchestral version, 1917, c 1918 by Durand et Cie., pp. 35–45. Reprinted by permission of the publisher, Theodore Presser Company, Sole Representative U.S.A.

a) *Don Quixote's theme*

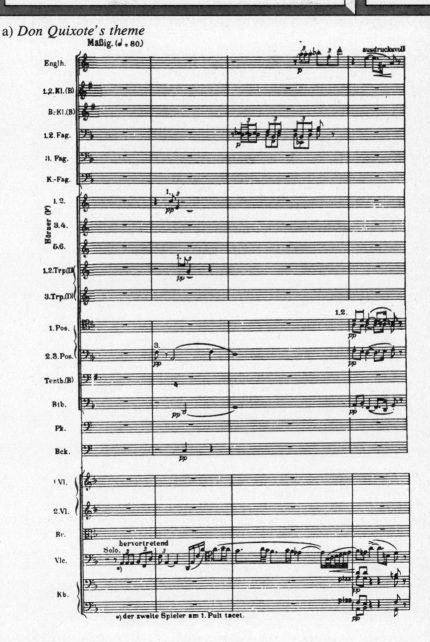

Reprinted from *Don Quixote, Symphonic Poem* (New York: Edition Peters, n.d.), pp. 37–59. By permission.

b) *Sancho Panza's theme*

d) *Variation II*

Igor Stravinsky *(1882–1971)*
Le Sacre du printemps (1913): **Danses des adolescentes**

143

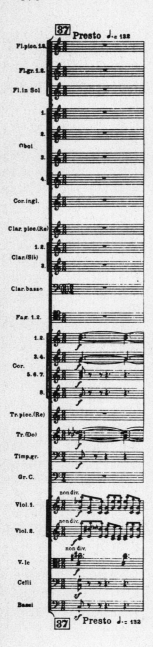

Igor Stravinsky
Symphony in Three Movements (1945): Andante (second movement)

144

Arnold Schoenberg (1874–1951)
Variationen für Orchester, Opus 31
(1928)

145

a) *Theme*

b) *Variation VI*

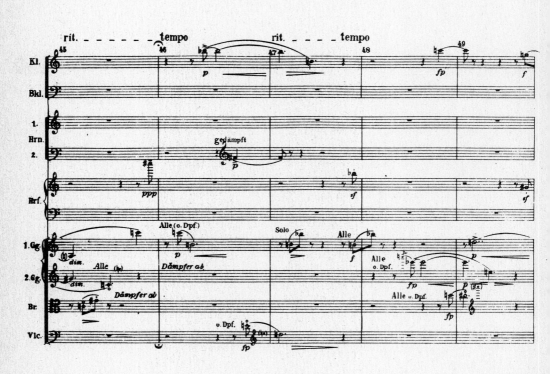

a) Original Shaker melody and text

b) Copland's setting and variations

148

Alexander Scriabin *(1872–1915)*
Vers la flamme, Poème pour piano,
Opus 72 *(1914)*

a) *No. 8, Nacht*

b) *No. 13,* Enthauptung

nie_der der Mond_____, das blan_ke Tür_kenschwert.

NIGHT

Finstre, schwarze Riesenfalter	Gloomy, black bats
Töteten der Sonne Glanz.	killed the radiant sun.
Ein geschlossnes Zauberbuch,	A sealed book of magic,
Ruht der Horizont—verschwiegen.	the horizon rests, taciturn.
Aus dem Qualm verlorner Tiefen	From the vapor of forgotten depths
Steigt ein Duft, Erinnrung mordend!	rises a fragrance, killing memory!
Finstre, schwarze Riesenfalter	Gloomy, black bats
Töteten der Sonne Glanz.	killed the radiant sun.
Und vom Himmel erdenwärts	And from heaven earthwards
Senken sich mit schweren Schwingen	they sink with ponderous oscillations—
Unsichtbar die Ungetüme	invisible, the monsters,
Auf die Menschenherzen nieder . . .	down to the hearts of men . . .
Finstre, schwarze Riesenfalter.	Gloomy, black bats.

DECAPITATION

Der Mond, ein blankes Türkenschwert,	The moon, a polished scimitar
Auf einen schwarzen Seidenkissen,	set on a black silken cushion,
Gespenstisch gross—dräut er hinab	ghostly vast, menaces downwards
Durch schmerzensdunkle Nacht.	through pain's dark night.
Pierrot irrt ohne Rast umher	Pierrot wanders about, restless,
Und starrt empor in Todesängsten	and stares on high in death-agony
Zum Mond, dem blanken Türkenschwert	at the moon, a polished scimitar
Auf einem schwarzen Seidenkissen.	set on a black silken cushion.
Es schlottern unter ihm die Knie,	His knees knock together under him,
Ohnmächtig bricht er jäh zusammen.	swooning, he collapses abruptly.
Er wähnt: es sause strafend schon	He fancies: let it whistle punishingly
Auf seinen Sündenhals hernieder	already down on his guilty neck,
Der Mond, das blanke Türkenschwert.	the moon, the polished scimitar.

ALBERT GIRAUD (1860–1929), translated from
the French by ERICH HARTLEBEN (1860–1905)

150 · Béla Bartók (1881–1945) · Music for String Instruments, Percussion and Celesta (1936): Adagio (third movement)

*) *Griffbezeichnung* / indique la manière de toucher

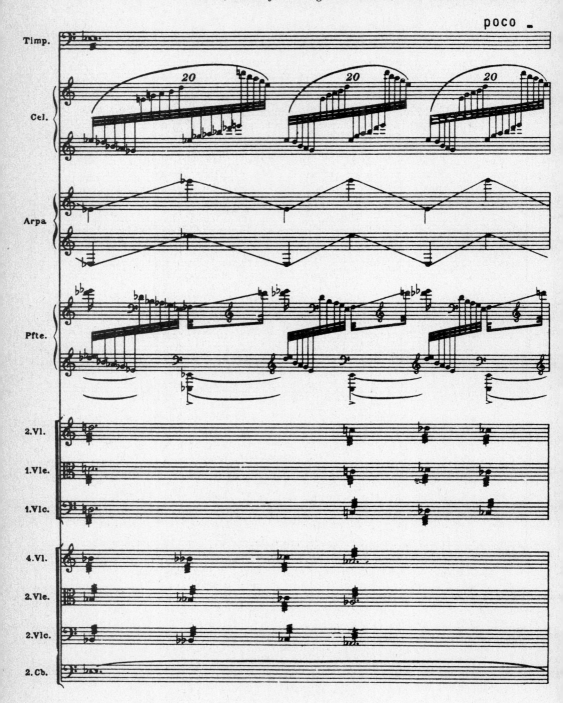

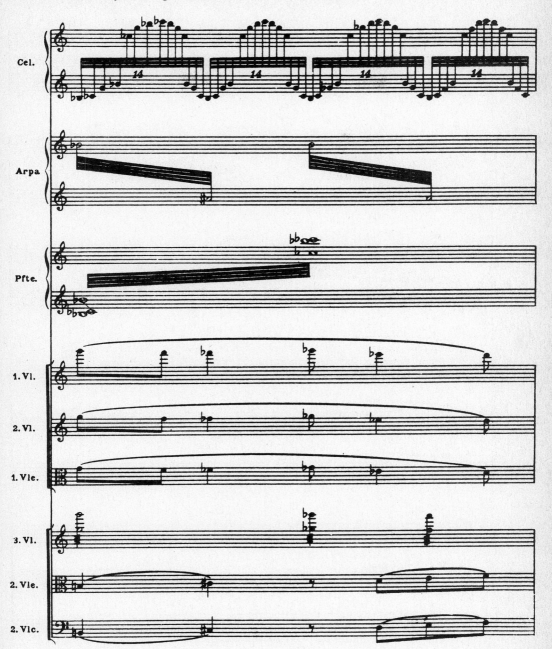

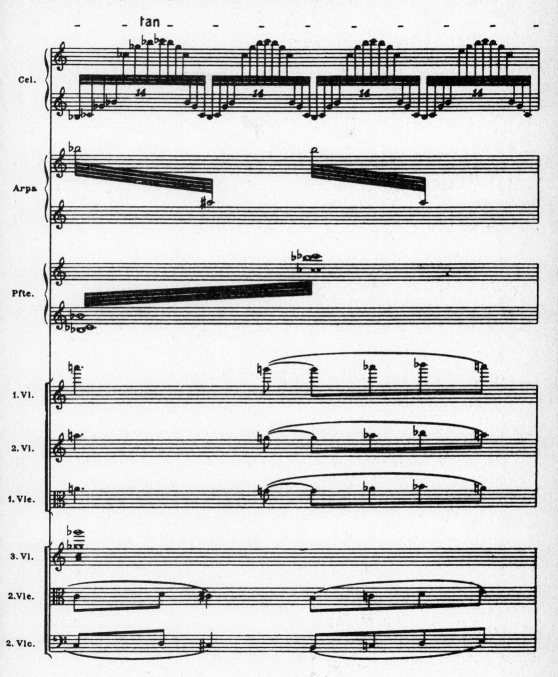

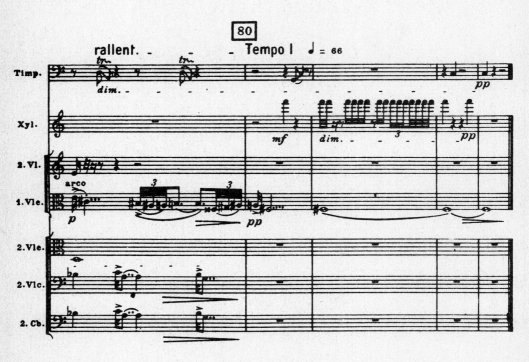

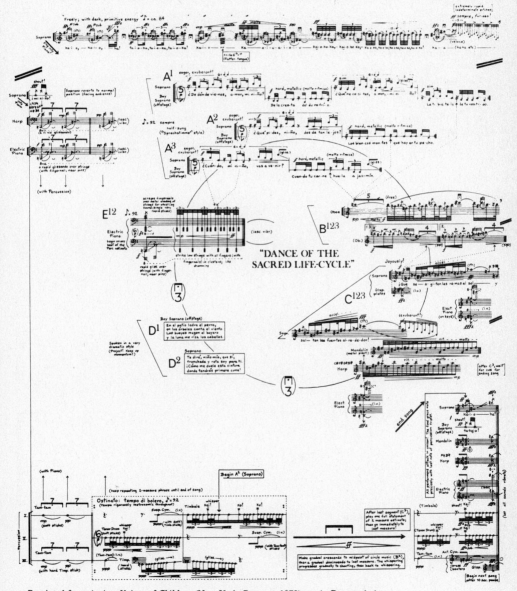

"DANCE OF THE
SACRED LIFE-CYCLE"

Reprinted from *Ancient Voices of Children* (New York: Peters, c1970), p. 4. By permission.

¿De dónde vienes, amor, mi niño?
De la cresta del duro frío.
¿Qué necesitas, amor, mi niño?
La tibia tela de tu vestido.

¿Qué pides, niño, desde tan lejos?

Los blancos montes que hay en tu pecho.
¿Cuándo, mi niño, vas a venir?
Cuando tu carne huela a jazmín.
¡Que se agiten las ramas al sol
Y salten las fuentes al rededor!

En el patio ladra el perro
En los árboles canta el viento.
Los bueyes mugen al boyero
Y la luna me riza los cabellos.

Te diré, niño mío, que sí,
Tronchada y rota soy para ti.
¡Cómo me duele esta cintura
donde tendrás primera cuna!

FREDERICO GARCÍA LORCA (1899–1936)

From where do you come, my love, my child?
From the crest of the hard frost.
What do you need, my love, my child?
The warm fabric of your dress.

What do you desire, my child, from so far
    away?
The white mountains of your breasts.
When, my child, are you going to come?
When your flesh smells of jasmine.
How the branches stir in the sun
and the fountains leap all around!

In the yard barks the dog;
in the trees sings the wind;
the oxen bellow at the ox driver
and the moon curls my hair.

I shall tell you, my child, yes.
I'm broken and torn because of you.
How this girdle hurts me
where you will have your first cradle!

<table>
<tr><td>

Olivier Messiaen (*b. 1908*)
Méditations sur le mystère de la Sainte Trinité (*1969*): Vif (fourth movement)

</td><td>

152

</td></tr>
</table>

All that we can know about God is summed up in these words at once so compact and simple: *he is;* words that we do not understand except in flashes, in rare and brief illuminations. Nearly all of this piece establishes a climate, preparing for the final vision. The strangeness of the bird calls chosen must evoke some unknown dimension . . . It is first of all the extraordinary cry of the Black Woodpecker (*Pic noir*), a rapid and discordant plaint that is heard in the forests of the Vosges or the high tops of the Larch trees and of the Piceas of the Dauphinese Alps. Two other primitive melodies: the call of the Ring Ouzel (*Merle à plastron*), and the little sad tolling bell in equal durations of the Tengmalm's Owl (*Chouette de Tengmalm*), heard in the Jura. Trilled clusters, a short trio passage evoking the Three Persons of the Holy Trinity. Then a long solo of the Song Thrush (*Grive musicienne*), with its thrice repeated themes on the *plein jeu* (principal chorus) and *clairon 4* (four-foot trumpet), and its changes of tone color and of attack (like pizzicato, water dropping, silk tearing). All of a sudden, towards the end of the piece, an organ fortissimo: chords in Iambic rhythm descending rapidly: this is the vision of Moses. "And the Lord ('I am') passed by before him, and proclaimed, The Lord ('I am, I am!') (*Exodus* 34:6). Grand silence. The Tengmalm's Owl recedes, expressing our pettiness overwhelmed by the lightning flash of the Holy Scripture.

(Prefatory note by the composer)

Éditions Musicales Alphonse Leduc, Paris, c 1973, pp. 29–36. Réproduit avec l'aimable autorisation de Alphonse Leduc & Cie., éditeurs et propriétaires en tous pays.

Comb. 1 R: fl., bourd., gambe ⃟ | Pos: cornet 5 rangs, cor de nuit 8– ⃟ | G: fl. harm., bourdon 8, bourdon 16– |

Très modéré (Merle à plastron)

(Chouette de Tengmalm)

Bien modéré   (bourdon 16, bourdon 8, seuls)

Comb. 6 R: fonds 16,8 – bombarde 16, trp. 8– ⃟ | Pos: fonds 16, 8, 4, mixtures, anches 16, 8, 4– ⃟ |
G: montre 8, prestant 4, plein jeu 5 rangs, cymbale 4 rangs – | Ped: fonds 16,8,32 – tir. R |

Vif
(en fusée)   (cri du Pic noir)
                    Un peu lent
                           (fermer
                    R: brusquement)

(en fusée)

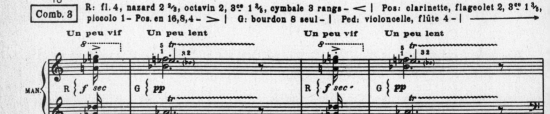

Comb. 3 R: fl. 4, nazard 2 ⅔, octavin 2, 3ᶜᵉ 1 ⅗, cymbale 3 rangs – ⃟ | Pos: clarinette, flageolet 2, 3ᶜᵉ 1 ⅗,
piccolo 1– Pos. en 16,8,4 – ⃟ | G: bourdon 8 seul– | Ped: violoncelle, flûte 4 – | ⟶

Un peu vif   Un peu lent   Un peu vif   Un peu lent

Comb. 5

35

R: bourdon 16, bourdon 8, nazard 2 ⅔, octavin 2 – ⟩ | Pos: fl. 4, nazard 2 ⅔, flageolet 2, 3ᶜᵉ 1 ⅗,
piccolo 1 – ⟨ | G: plein jeu 5 rangs – clairon 4 – |

(grand solo de Grive musicienne)

(très sec, comme des pizzi)

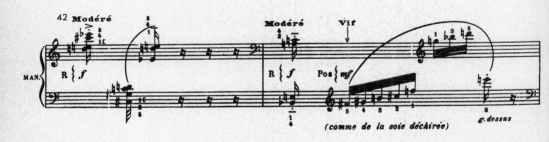

(comme de la soie déchirée)

g. dessus

(très sec, comme des pizzi)

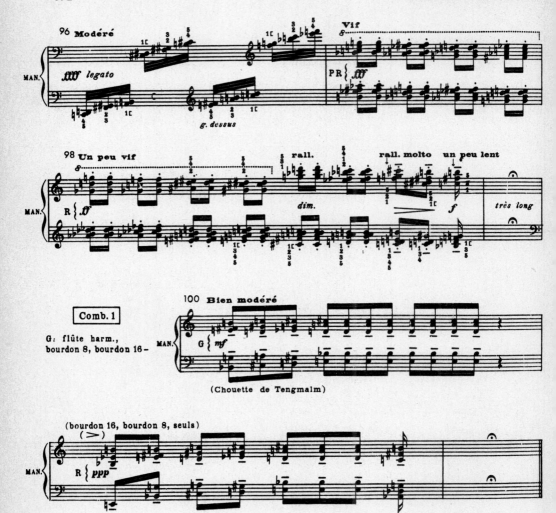

(Chouette de Tengmalm)

thym!

Quasi Adagio. ♩=68

dolce

Tour-ne devers le po - è - te dont les yeux sont pleins d'a-

Allegro moderato. ♩=96

- mour

L'a-lou - et - te mon-te au ciel a-vec le

Avant que tu ne t'en ailles,
Pâle étoile du matin,
—Mille cailles
Chantent, chantent dans le thym.—

Tourne devers le poète,
Dont les yeux sont pleins d'amour,
—L'alouette
Monte au ciel avec le jour.—

Tourne ton regard que noie
L'aurore dans son azur;
—Quelle joie
Parmi les champs de blé mûr!—

Et fais luire ma pensée
Là-bas, bien loin, oh! bien loin!
—La rosée
Gaîment brille sur le foin.—

Dans le doux rêve où s'agite
Ma vie endormie encor . . .
—Vite, vite,
Car voici le soleil d'or.—

        PAUL VERLAINE (1844–96)

Before you go,
pale star of morning—
a thousand quails
sing, sing in the thyme.

Turn toward the poet,
whose eyes are filled with love—
the lark
climbs to the sky with the day.

Turn your gaze, that
the dawn drowns in its azure hue;—
what joy
in the fields of ripe wheat!

Then make my thought shine
down there, quite far, o, quite far!—
The dew
merrily sparkles in the hay.

In the sweet dream in which stirs
my life, still asleep. . .—
quick, quick,
for here is the golden sun.

See p. 509, Debussy, *Nuages*, where the accompaniment figure of measure 16 is borrowed. The present edition, based on that published by N. A. Rimsky-Korsakov in 1908, is identical musically to that printed by W. Bessel & Co., St. Petersburg, in 1874; the Russian text, omitted in 1908, has been restored.

чах и.ной ден.ни.цы, Во.о.бра. же.ни.е вер.тит го
-yons des vieil - les heu - res, mon coeur s'at - tar.de a feuil-le - ter les

дов у . тра.чен.ных стра. ни . цы. Как буд.то вновь вды . ха . я
pa - ges des an-nées dé - fun-tes et j'y res - pire un lent poi-

яд _____ Ве . сен.них, страст. ных
-son. _____ Prin - temps pas - sés, ar -

шум их ста_рой бол_тов_ни у_же не влас_тен на_ до мно_ю. Лишь

par_ lent un lan_gage an_cien, au_quel mon á_me res_te clo_se. Voi-

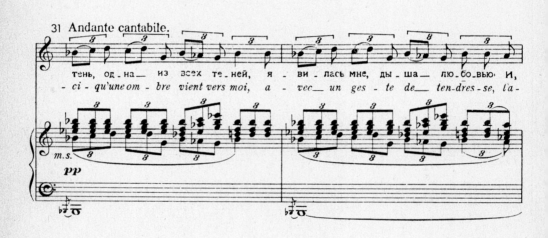

тень, од_на_ из всех те_ней, я_ ви_лась мне, ды_ша лю_бо_вью. И,

-ci qu'une om_bre vient vers moi, a_vec_ un ges_te de_ ten_dres_se, l'a-

вер_ный друг ми_нув_ших дней, Скло_ни_лась ти_хо к из_го_ло_вью. И

-mante fi_dè_le d'au_tre fois s'in_cline à mon che_vet,_ mu_et_te; d'un

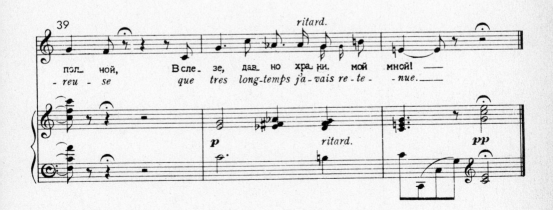

Les jours de fête sont finis,
Dans le silence, tout repose, tout s'endort.
L'ombre de la nuit de mai se glisse sur la ville,

Mais moi je ne puis m'endormir . . .
Car aux rayons des vieilles heures,
Mon coeur s'attarde à feuilleter
Les pages des années défuntes,
Et j'y respire un lent poison.
Printemps passés, ardeurs, extases
Revient dans mon coeur troublé.
L'espoir, les rêves, les chimères,
Hélas! me sont tous apparus.
Je souffre en voyant ces fantômes!
Ils parlent un langage ancien,
Auquel mon âme reste close.
Voici qu'une ombre vient vers moi,
Avec un geste de tendresse,
L'amante fidèle d'autrefois
S'incline à mon chevet, muette;
D'un seul élan, je lui tendis mon coeur,
En une larme timide, silencieuse, bien-
    heureuse,
Que très longtemps j'avais retenue.

The festive days are over.
In the silence, all rest, all sleep.
The darkness of the May night slips through
    the city,

but I cannot fall asleep . . .
for in the rays of the aging hours,
my heart tarries as it leafs
through the pages of the deceased years,
and I breathe a slow poison.
Spring gone, ardors, extasies
return to my troubled heart.
Hope, dreams, fancies,
alas, all appeared to me.
I suffer as I see these phantoms.
They speak an ancient language,
to which my soul is deaf.
Here comes a shadow towards me;
with a gesture of tenderness
the faithful lover of yesteryears
bends over the bolster of my bed, mute;
with a bound, I extend to her my soul,
and a timid tear, silent, happy enough,

that for a long time I had held in.

French translation from the Russian
by MICHEL DIMITRI CALVOCORESSI

Maestoso (*but with energy and not too slowly*)

In Flanders fields the pop - pies blow, Be - tween the cross - es,
(Baritone or Male Chorus)

row on row— That mark our place; And in the sky the larks still bravely sing-ing fly, Scarce

Poem by JOHN MCCRAE

*) Triller ohne Nachschlag

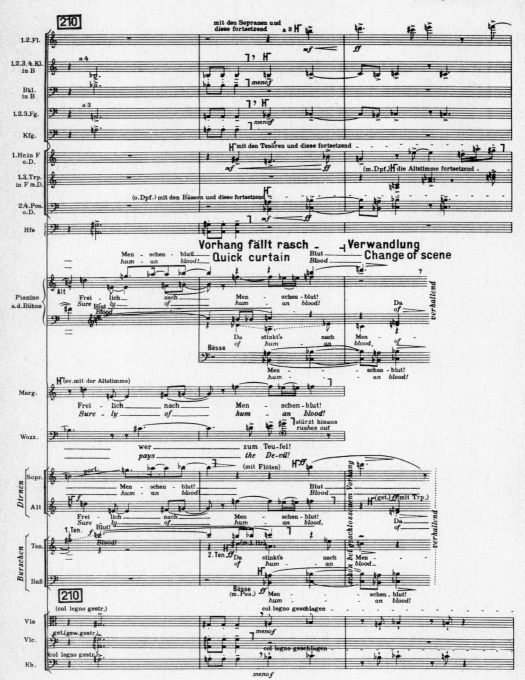

Adapted by the composer from the play by GEORGE BUECHNER (1813-37)

157

Paul Hindemith (1895–1963)
Mathis der Maler: Sechstes Bild

Very slow, free in measure
Sehr langsam, frei im Zeitmaß

First performance 1938. Reprinted from *Mathis der Maler* (Mainz: B. Schott's Söhne, c1970), pp. 241–57. Used by permission of European American Music Distributors Corp. Sole U.S. Agent for B. Schotts Söhne.

Sixth Tableau

The Odenwald. A region with tall trees in the late twilight. Regina rushes in, Mathis close behind her.

MATHIS

Du wirst mich verlieren. Es ist zu lange her,	You almost lost me. It was too long ago
Dass ich so jung war wie du und so schnell.	that I was as young and as fast as you.

REGINA

Lass uns doch	Let us then
Weiterlaufen.	go on.

MATHIS

Wohin willst du in der Nacht?	Where would you go in the dark?

REGINA

Wer	Who could ever
Hat mir je gesagt, wohin der Weg geht? Noch	tell me where the path leads? Yet
Immer drangen wir ins Unbekannte.	we always hurry into the unknown.

MATHIS

Keiner jagt	No one chases
Uns mehr.	us any more.

REGINA

Wie weisst du das? Der liebste Vater, er verstand	How do you know that? My dearest father – he understood
Mich ohne Worte, er führte mich zart an der Hand.	me without words; he led me tenderly by the hand.
Und nur ein mal, zuletzt, liess er	And only once, for the last time, did he leave me
Mich allein zurück. Seit ich ihn tot liegen sah,	alone behind. For then I saw him lying dead
Im Blute, mit offnen Augen, die wie ein	in blood, with eyes open, as if
Wunder des Himmels Schwärze anstarrten, mit den angstvoll	he were staring at the mystery of heaven's darkness, his pained
Verkrallten Händen, schüttelt mich die Angst, dass der	hands twisted. I tremble with anxiety for fear
Tote Mann mir folgt. Er holt mich ein, ist nah,	the dead man is following me. He is overtaking me; he is nearby.
Ergreift mich. Und wie sehnlich wünschte ich, mein	He grabs me. How ardently I wish that
Herz bei ihm in Ruhe zu betten. Soll mich Sehnsucht, soll	he would put my heart to rest. Shall the longing
Mich Entsetzten lähmen? Sage mir: wo ist er?	and fear cripple me? Tell me: where is he?
Versinkt ein Toter, wird er erhoben?	A dead man sinks down; will he be lifted up?
Lass mich nicht allein!	Do not leave me alone.

MATHIS

Mein Töchterlein, zusammen bleiben wir.	My little daughter, we shall remain together.

(he kisses her)

Beruhige dich. Lege dich zum Schlaf auf meinen Mantel.	Now have a rest. Lie down to sleep on my cloak.

(He spreads his cloak to make a bed, settles her down, and comforting her, sits down beside her).

Wie mürbe ist des Alters Pein,
Masslos das Leid der Jugend.—Alte Märchen woben
Uns fromme Bilder, die ein Widerscheinen
Des Höheren sind. Ihr Sinn ist dir
Fern, du kannst ihn nur erahnen.
Und frömmer noch reden
Zu uns die Töne, wenn Musik, in Einfalt hier
Geboren, die Spur himmlischer Herkunft trägt.
Sieh, wie ein Schar von Engeln ewige Bahnen
In irdischen Wegen abwandelt. Wie spürt man jeden
Versenkt in sein mildes Amt. Der eine geigt
Mit wundersam gesperrtem Arm, den Bogen wägt
Er zart, damit nicht eines wenigen Schattens Rauheit
Den linden Lauf trübe. Ein andrer streicht
Gehobnen Blicks aus Saiten seine Freude.
Verhaftet scheint der dritte dem fernen Geläute
Seiner Seele und achtet leicht des Spiels. Wie bereit
Er ist, zugleich zu hören und zu bedient.

How weary is the pain of old age,
boundless the sorrow of youth!—Old tales they wove:
to us innocent images that are a reflection
of higher things. Their sense
eludes you; you can only surmise it.
And more uncannily still
do tones speak to us when music strikes up,
bearing a sign of heavenly origin.
See how a troop of angels wanders through eternal paths
in an earthly direction. See how each one
is engrossed in his tender task! One fiddles:
with wonderfully outstretched arm he balances the bow.
He fondles it so that not a shadow of coarseness
will disturb its gentle course. Another strokes
uplifted glances from the strings of his joy.
A third seems to listen to the ringing of bells
in his soul. How ready
he is both to hear and to serve.

REGINA

Es sungen drei Engel ein süssen Gesang,
Der weit in den hohen Himmel erklang.

Three angels sing a sweet song
that resounds widely through those high heavens.

MATHIS

Ihr Kleid selbst musiziert mit ihnen.
In schillernden Federn schwirrt der Töne Gegenspiel.
Ein leichter Panzer unirdischen Metalls erglüht,
Berührt vom Wogen des Klanges wie vom Beben
Bewegten Herzens. Und im Zusammenklang viel
Bunter Lichterkreise wird aus kaum gehörtem Lied
Auf wunderbare Art sichtbares Formenleben.

Even their garments make music
as their iridescent feathers whir a counter-voice.
A light coat of mail of unearthly metal glows,
shimmering with the waves of sound as with the trembling
of an agitated heart. And through the harmony
of countless bursts of color will form from a barely heard song
a wonderful kind of visible living form.

REGINA

Es eint sich mit ihnen der himmlische Chor,
Sie singen Gott und den Heiligen vor.

Joining with them is the heavenly choir.
They sing to God and the saints.

MATHIS
(Light has fallen).

Wie diese ihr klingendes Werk verrichten,
So beten andre. Mit weichen Füssen treten
Sie auf die weicheren Stufen der Töne. Und du
Weisst nicht: musizieren, die Gebete dichten

Oder hörst du der Musikanten Beten.
Ist so Musik Gebet geworden, hört lauschend
    zu
Natur. Ein Rest des Schimmers solcher
    Sphären
Mög unser dunkles Tun verklären.

While some attend to their sonorous duties,
others pray. With fleet feet they
descend the delicate steps of tones. And
you do not know whether, making music, they
    invent prayers
or whether you hear the musicians praying.
Has music, then, become prayer, as it imitates
    the harmony
of nature? A residue of splendor of those
    spheres
may brighten up our dark path.

REGINA
(falling asleep)

Die Welt ist erfüllt von göttlichem Schall,
Im Herzen der Menschen ein Widerhall.

The world is filled with a godly ringing;
in the hearts of men sounds the echo.

Benjamin Britten *(1913–76)*
Peter Grimes, Opus 33 *(1945)*: Act III, *To hell with all your mercy*

158

BALSTRODE: *(Crossing to lift Peter up)* Come on, I'll help you with the boat.
ELLEN: No!
BALSTRODE: Sail out till you lose sight of the Moot Hall.   Then sink the boat.   D'you hear? Sink her. Good-
                 bye Peter.

There is a crunch of shingle as Balstrode leads Peter down to his boat, and helps him push it out.   After a short pause, he returns, takes Ellen by the arm, and leads her away.

             Dawn slowly begins and the Borough slowly comes to life.   Some stragglers of the manhunt go

53 **Lento e tranquillo** *(come prima)*

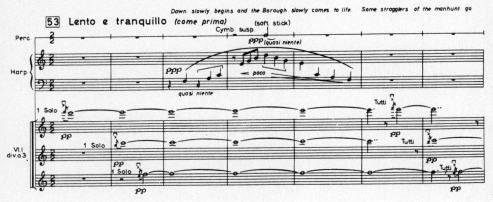

End of Opera

Libretto by MONTAGU SLATER on a poem by GEORGE CRABBE

Instrumental Names and Abbreviations

The following tables set forth the English, Italian, German, and French names used for the various musical instruments in these scores, and their respective abbreviations.

WOODWINDS

English	Italian	German	French
Piccolo (Picc.)	Flauto piccolo (Fl. Picc.)	Kleine Flöte (Kl. Fl.)	Petite flûte
Flute (Fl.)	Flauto (Fl.); Flauto grande (Fl. gr.)	Grosse Flöte (Fl. gr.)	Flûte (Fl.)
Alto flute	Flauto contralto (fl.c-alto)	Altflöte	Flûte en sol
Oboe (Ob.)	Oboe (Ob.)	Hoboe (Hb.); Oboe (Ob.)	Hautbois (Hb.)
English horn (E. H.)	Corno inglese (C. or Cor. ingl., C.i.)	Englisches Horn	Cor anglais (C. A.)
Sopranino clarinet	Clarinetto piccolo (clar. picc.)		
Clarinet (C., Cl., Clt., Clar.)	Clarinetto (Cl. Clar.)	Klarinette (Kl.)	Clarinette (Cl.)
Bass clarinet (B. Cl.)	Clarinetto basso (Cl. b., Cl. basso, Clar. basso)	Bass Klarinette (Bkl.)	Clarinette basse (Cl. bs.)
Bassoon (Bsn., Bssn.)	Fagotto (Fag., Fg.)	Fagott (Fag., Fg.)	Basson (Bssn.)
Contrabassoon (C. Bsn.)	Contrafagotto (Cfg., C. Fag., Cont. F.)	Kontrafagott (Kfg.)	Contrebasson (C. bssn.)

BRASS

English	Italian	German	French
French horn (Hr., Hn.)	Corno (Cor., C.)	Horn (Hr.) [pl. Hörner (Hrn.)]	Cor; Cor à pistons
Trumpet (Tpt., Trpt., Trp., Tr.)	Tromba (Tr.)	Trompete (Tr., Trp.)	Trompette (Tr.)

English	Italian	German	French
Trumpet in D	Tromba piccola (Tr. picc.)		
Cornet	Cornetta	Kornett	Cornet à pistons (C. à p., Pist.)
Trombone (Tr., Tbe., Trb., Trm., Trbe.)	Trombone [pl. Tromboni (Tbni., Trni.)]	Posaune.(Ps., Pos.)	Trombone (Tr.)
Tuba (Tb.)	Tuba (Tb, Tbaı)	Tuba (Tb.)	Tuba (Tb.)

PERCUSSION

English	Italian	German	French
Percussion (Perc.)	Percussione	Schlagzeug (Schlag.)	Batterie (Batt.)
Kettledrums (K. D.)	Timpani (Timp., Tp.)	Pauken (Pk.)	Timbales (Timb.)
Snare drum (S. D.)	Tamburo piccolo (Tamb. picc.) Tamburo militare (Tamb. milit.)	Kleine Trommel (Kl. Tr.)	Caisse claire (C. cl.), Caisse roulante Tambour militaire (Tamb. milit.)
Bass drum (B. drum)	Gran cassa (Gr. Cassa, Gr. C., G. C.)	Grosse Trommel (Gr. Tr.)	Grosse caisse (Gr. c.)
Cymbals (Cym., Cymb.)	Piatti (P., Ptti., Piat.)	Becken (Beck.)	Cymbales (Cym.)
Tam-Tam (Tam-T.)			
Tambourine (Tamb.)	Tamburino (Tamb.)	Schellentrommel, Tamburin	Tambour de Basque (T. de B., Tamb. de Basque)
Triangle (Trgl., Tri.)	Triangolo (Trgl.)	Triangel	Triangle (Triang.)
Glockenspiel (Glocken.)	Campanelli (Cmp.)	Glockenspiel	Carillon
Bells (Chimes)	Campane (Cmp.)	Glocken	Cloches
Antique Cymbals	Crotali Piatti antichi	Antiken Zimbeln	Cymbales antiques
Sleigh Bells	Sonagli (Son.)	Schellen	Grelots
Xylophone (Xyl.)	Xilofono	Xylophon	Xylophone

STRINGS

English	Italian	German	French
Violin (V., Vl., Vln, Vi.)	Violino (V., Vl., Vln.)	Violine (V., Vl., Vln.) Geige (Gg.)	Violon (V., Vl., Vln.)
Viola (Va., Vl., *pl.* Vas.)	Viola (Va., Vla.) *pl.* Viole (Vle.)	Bratsche (Br.)	Alto (A.)
Violoncello, Cello (Vcl., Vc.)	Violoncello (Vc., Vlc., Vcllo.)	Violoncell (Vc., Vlc.)	Violoncelle (Vc.)
Double bass (D. Bs.)	Contrabasso (Cb., C. B.) *pl.* Contrabassi or Bassi (C. Bassi, Bi.)	Kontrabass (Kb.)	Contrebasse (C. B.)

OTHER INSTRUMENTS

English	Italian	German	French
Harp (Hp., Hrp.)	Arpa (A., Arp.)	Harfe (Hrf.)	Harpe (Hp.)
Piano	Pianoforte (P.-f., Pft.)	Klavier	Piano
Celesta (Cel.)			
Harpsichord	Cembalo	Cembalo	Clavecin
Harmonium (Harmon.)			
Organ (Org.)	Organo	Orgel	Orgue

APPENDIX B

Glossary

a. The phrases *a 2, a 3* (etc.) indicate that the part is to be played in unison by 2, 3 (etc.) players; when a simple number (1., 2., etc.) is placed over a part, it indicates that only the first (second, etc.) player in that group should play.

abdämpfen. To mute.

aber. But.

accelerando (acc.). Growing faster.

accompagnato (accomp.). In a continuo part, this indicates that the chord-playing instrument resumes (*cf. tasto solo*).

adagio. Slow, leisurely.

a demi-jeu. Half-organ; i.e., softer registration.

ad libitum (ad lib.). An indication giving the performer liberty to: (1) vary from strict tempo; (2) include or omit the part of some voice or instrument; (3) include a cadenza of his own invention.

agitato. Agitated, excited.

alla breve. A time signature (¢) indicating, in the sixteenth century, a single breve per two-beat measure; in later music, the half note rather than the quarter is the unit of beat.

allargando (allarg.). Growing broader.

alle, alles. All, every, each.

allegretto. A moderately fast tempo (between allegro and andante).

allegro. A rapid tempo (between allegretto and presto).

alto, altus (A.). The deeper of the two main divisions of women's (or boys') voices.

am Frosch. At the heel (of a bow).

am Griffbrett. Play near, or above, the fingerboard of a string instrument.

amoroso. Loving, amorous.

am Steg. On the bridge (of a string instrument).

ancora. Again.

andante. A moderately slow tempo (between adagio and allegretto).

animato,animé. Animated.

a piacere. The execution of the passage is left to the performer's discretion.

arco. Played with the bow.

arpeggiando, arpeggiato (arpeg.). Played in harp style, i.e. the notes of the chord played in quick succession rather than simultaneously.

assai. Very.

a tempo. At the (basic) tempo.

attacca. Begin what follows without pausing.

auf dem. On the (as in *auf dem G*, on the G string).

Auftritt. Scene.

Ausdruck. Expression.

ausdrucksvoll. With expression.

Auszug. Arrangement.

baguettes. Drumsticks (*baguettes de bois, baguettes timbales de bois*, wooden drumsticks or kettledrum sticks; *baguettes d'éponge*, sponge-headed drumsticks; *baguettes midures*, semi-hard drumsticks; *baguettes dures*, hard drumsticks; *baguettes timbales en feutre*, felt-headed kettledrum sticks).

bariton. Brass instrument.

bass, basso, bassus (B.). The lowest male voice.

Begleitung. Accompaniment.

belebt. Animated.

beruhigen. To calm, to quiet.

bewegt. Agitated.

bewegter. More agitated.

bien. Very.

breit. Broadly.

breiter. More broadly.

Bühne. Stage.

cadenza. An extended passage for solo instrument in free, improvisatory style.

calando. Diminishing in volume and speed.

cambiare. To change.

cantabile (cant.). In a singing style.

cantando. In a singing manner.

canto. Voice (as in *col canto*, a direction for the accompaniment to follow the solo part in tempo and expression).

cantus. An older designation for the highest part in a vocal work.

chiuso. Stopped, in horn playing.

col, colla, coll'. With the.

come prima, come sopra. As at first; as previously.

come. Like, as.

comodo. Comfortable, easy.

con. With.

Continuo (Con.). A method of indicating an accompanying part by the bass notes only, together with figures designating the chords to be played above them. In general practice, the chords are played on a lute, harpsichord or organ, while, often, a viola da gamba or cello doubles the bass notes.

contratenor. In earlier music, the name given to the third voice part which was added to the basic two voice texture of discant and tenor, having the same range as the tenor which it frequently crosses.

corda. String; for example, *seconda (2a) corda* is the second string (the A string on the violin).

coro. Chorus.

coryphée. Leader of a ballet or chorus.

countertenor. Male alto, derived from *contratenor altus.*

crescendo (cresc.). Increasing in volume.

da capo (D.C.). Repeat from the beginning, usually up to the indication *Fine* (end).

daher. From there.

dal segno. Repeat from the sign.

Dämpfer (Dpf.). Mute.

decrescendo (decresc., decr.). Decreasing in volume.

delicato. Delicate, soft.

dessus. Treble.

détaché. With a broad, vigorous bow stroke, each note bowed singly.

deutlich. Distinctly.

diminuendo, diminuer (dim., dimin.). Decreasing in volume.

discantus. Improvised counterpoint to an existing melody.

divisés, divisi (div.). Divided; indicates that the instrumental group should be divided into two or more parts to play the passage in question.

dolce. Sweet and soft.

dolcemente. Sweetly.

dolcissimo (dolciss.). Very sweet.

Doppelgriff. Double stop.

doppelt. Twice.

doppio movimento. Twice as fast.

doux. Sweet.

drängend. Pressing on.

e. And.

Echoton. Like an echo.

éclatant. Sparkling, brilliant.

einleiten. To lead into.

Encore. Again.

en dehors. Emphasized.

en fusée. Dissolving in.

erschütterung. A violent shaking, deep emotion.

espressione intensa. Intense expression.

espressivo (espress., espr.). Expressive.

et. And.

etwas. Somewhat, rather.

expressif (express.). Expressive.

falsetto. Male singing voice in which notes above the ordinary range are obtained artificially.

falsobordone. Four-part harmonization of psalm tones with mainly root-position chords.

fauxbourdon (faulx bourdon). Three-part harmony in which the chant melody in the treble is accompanied by two lower voices, one in parallel sixths, and the other improvised a fourth below the melody.

fermer brusquement. To close abruptly.

fine. End, close.

flatterzunge, flutter-tongue. A special tonguing technique for wind instruments, producing a rapid trill-like sound.

flüchtig. Fleeting, transient.

fois. Time (as in *premier fois,* first time).

forte (f). Loud.

fortissimo (ff). Very loud (*fff* indicates a still louder dynamic).

fortsetzend. Continuing.

forza. Force.

frei. Free.

fugato. A section of a composition fugally treated.

funebre. Funereal, mournful.

fuoco. Fire, spirit.

furioso. Furious.

ganz. Entirely, altogether.

gebrochen. Broken.

gedehnt. Held back.

gemächlich. Comfortable.

Generalpause (G.P.). Rest for the complete orchestra.

geschlagen. Struck.

geschwinder. More rapid, swift.

gesprochen. Spoken.

gesteigert. Intensified.

gestopft (chiuso). Stopped; for the notes of a horn obtained by placing the hand in the bell.

gestrichen (gestr.). Bowed.

gesungen. Sung.

geteilt (get.). Divided; indicates that the instrumental group should be divided into two parts to play the passage in question.

gewöhnlich (gew., gewöhnl.). Usual, customary.

giusto. Moderate.

gleichmässig. Equal, symmetrical.

gli altri. The others.

glissando (gliss.). Rapidly gliding over strings or keys, producing a scale run.

grande. Large, great.

grave. Slow, solemn; deep, low.

gravement. Gravely, solemnly.

grazioso. Graceful.

grossem. Large, big.

H⌐ . Hauptstimme, the most important voice in the texture.

Halbe. Half.

Halt. Stop, hold.

harmonic (harm.). A flute-like sound produced on a

string instrument by lightly touching the string with the finger instead of pressing it down.

Hauptzeitmass. Original tempo.
heftiger. More passionate, violent.
hervortretend. Prominently.
Holz. Woodwinds.
hörbar. Audible.

immer. Always.
impetuoso. Impetuous, violent.
istesso tempo. The same tempo, as when the duration of the beat remains unaltered despite meter change.

klagend. Lamenting.
klangvoll. Sonorous, full-sounding.
klingen lassen. Allow to sound.
kräftig. Strong, forceful.
kurz. Short.
kurzer. Shorter.

laissez vibrer. Let vibrate; an indication to the player of a harp, cymbal, etc., that the sound must not be damped.
langsam. Slow.
langsamer. Slower.
largamente. Broadly.
larghetto. Slightly faster than largo.
largo. A very slow tempo.
lebhaft. Lively.
legato. Performed without any perceptible interruption between notes.
leggéro, leggiero (legg.). Light and graceful.
legno. The wood of the bow (*col legno tratto,* bowed with the wood; *col legno battuto,* tapped with the wood; *col legno gestrich,* played with the wood).
leidenschaftlich. Passionate, vehement.
lent. Slow.
lentamente. Slowly.
lento. A slow tempo (between andante and largo).
l.h. Abbreviation for "left hand."
lié. Tied.

ma. But.
maestoso. Majestic.
maggiore. Major key.
main. Hand (*droite,* right; *gauche,* left).
marcatissimo (marcatiss.). With very marked emphasis.
marcato (marc.). Marked, with emphasis.
marcia. March.
marqué. Marked, with emphasis.
mässig. Moderate.
mean. Middle part of a polyphonic composition.
meno. Less.
mezza voce. With half the voice power.
mezzo forte (mf). Moderately loud.
mezzo piano (mp). Moderately soft.
minore. In the minor mode.

minuetto. Minuet.
mit. With
M. M. Metronome; followed by an indication of the setting for the correct tempo.
moderato, modéré. At a moderate tempo.
molto. Very, much.
mosso. Rapid.
motetus. In medieval polyphonic music, a voice part above the tenor; generally, the first additional part to be composed.
moto. Motion.
muta, mutano. Change the tuning of the instrument as specified.

N⎯. Nebenstimme, the second most important voice in the texture.
Nachslag. Auxiliary note (at end of trill).
nehmen (nimmt). To take.
neue. New.
nicht, non. Not.
noch. Still, yet.

octava (okt., 8va). Octave; if not otherwise qualified, means the notes marked should be played an octave higher than written.
ohne (o.). Without.
open. In brass instruments, the opposite of muted. In string instruments, refers to the unstopped string (i.e. sounding at its full length).
ordinario, ordinairement (ordin., ord.). In the usual way (generally cancelling an instruction to play using some special technique).
ôtez les sourdines. Remove the mutes.

parlando. A singing style with the voice approximating speech.
parte. Part (*colla parte,* the accompaniment is to follow the soloist in tempo).
passione. Passion.
pause. Rest.
pedal (ped., P.). In piano music, indicates that the damper pedal should be depressed; an asterisk indicates the point of release (brackets below the music are also used to indicate pedalling). On an organ, the pedals are a keyboard played with the feet.
perdendosi. Gradually dying away.
peu. Little, a little.
pianissimo (pp). Very soft (*ppp* indicates a still softer dynamic).
piano (p). Soft.
più. More.
pizzicato (pizz.). The string plucked with the finger.
plötzlich. Suddenly, immediately.
plus. More.
pochissimo (pochiss.). Very little.
poco. Little, a little.
poco a poco. Little by little.

ponticello (*pont.*). The bridge (of a string instrument).

portato. Performance manner between legato and staccato.

prenez. Take up.

près de la table. On the harp, the plucking of the strings near the soundboard.

prestissimo. Very fast.

presto. A very quick tempo (faster than allegro).

prima. First.

principale (*pr.*). Principal, solo.

quasi. Almost, as if.

quasi niente. Almost nothing, i.e. as softly as possible.

quintus. An older designation for the fifth part in a vocal work.

rallentando (*rall.*, *rallent.*). Growing slower.

rasch. Quick.

recitative (*recit.*). A vocal style designed to imitate and emphasize the natural inflections of speech.

rinforzando (*rinf.*). Sudden accent on a single note or chord.

ritardando (*rit.*, *ritard.*). Gradually slackening in speed.

ritmico. Rhythmical.

rubato. A certain elasticity and flexibility of tempo, speeding up and slowing down, according to the requirements of the music.

ruhig. Calm.

ruhiger. More calmly.

saltando (*salt.*). An indication to the string player to bounce the bow off the string by playing with short, quick bow-strokes.

sans. Without.

scherzando (*scherz.*). Playfully.

schleppend. Dragging.

schnell. Fast.

schneller. Faster.

schon. Already.

schwerer. Heavier, more difficult.

schwermütig. Dejected, sad.

sec., *secco*. Dry, simple.

segno. Sign in form of :S: indicating the beginning and end of a section to be repeated.

segue. (1) Continue to the next movement without pausing; (2) continue in the same manner.

sehr. Very.

semplice. Simple, in a simple manner.

sempre. Always, continually.

senza. Without.

senza mis[*ura*]. Free of regular meter.

serpent. Bass of the cornett family.

seulement. Only.

sforzando, *sforzato* (*sfz*, *sf*). With sudden emphasis.

simile. In a similar manner.

sino al . . . Up to the . . . (usually followed by a new tempo marking, or by a dotted line indicating a terminal point).

sombre. Dark, somber.

son. Sound.

sonore. Sonorous, with full tone.

sopra. Above; in piano music, used to indicate that one hand must pass above the other.

soprano (*Sop.*, *S.*) The voice with the highest range.

sordino (*sord.*). Mute.

sostenendo, *sostenuto* (*sost.*). Sustained.

sotto voce. In an undertone, subdued, under the breath.

sourdine. Mute.

soutenu. Sustained.

spiccato. With a light bouncing motion of the bow.

spiritoso. Lively, witty.

sprechstimme (*sprechst.*). Speaking voice.

staccato (*stacc.*). Detached, separated, abruptly disconnected.

stentando, *stentato* (*stent.*). Delaying, retarding.

Stimme. Voice.

strepitoso, *strepito*. Noisy, boisterous.

stretto. In a non-fugal composition, indicates a concluding section at an increased speed.

stringendo (*string.*). Quickening.

subito (*sub.*). Suddenly, immediately.

sul. On the (as in *sul G,* on the G string).

suono. Sound, tone.

superius. The uppermost part.

sur. On.

Takt. Bar, beat.

tasto solo. In a continuo part, this indicates that only the string instrument plays; the chord-playing instrument is silent.

tempo primo (*tempo I*). At the original tempo.

tendrement. Tenderly.

tenerezza. Tenderness.

tenor, *tenore* (*T.*, *ten.*). High male voice or part.

tenuto (*ten.*). Held, sustained.

touche. Fingerboard or fret (of a string instrument).

tranquillo. Quiet, calm.

trauernd. Mournfully.

treble. Soprano voice or range.

tremolo (*trem*). On string instruments, a quick reiteration of the same tone, produced by a rapid up-and-down movement of the bow; also a rapid alteration between two different notes.

très. Very.

trill (*tr.*). The rapid alternation of a given note with the note above it. In a drum part it indicates rapid alternating strokes with two drumsticks.

triplum. In medieval polyphonic music, a second voice part added above the tenor or chant.

tristement. Sadly.

troppo. Too much.

tutti. Literally, "all"; usually means all the instru-

ments in a given category as distinct from a
solo part.

übertönend. Drowning out.
unison (unis.). The same notes or melody played by
several instruments at the same pitch. Often
used to emphasize that a phrase is not to be
divided among several players.
Unterbrechung. Interruption, suspension.

veloce. Fast.
verhalten. Restrained, held back.
verklingen lassen. To let die away.
Verwandlung. Change of scene.
verzweiflungsvoll. Full of despair.
vibrato. Slight fluctuation of pitch around a sustained tone.
vif. Lively.

vigoroso. Vigorous, strong.
vivace. Quick, lively.
voce. Voice.
volti. Turn over (the page).
Vorhang auf. Curtain up.
Vorhang fällt, Vorhang zu. Curtain down.
voriges. Preceding.
vorwärts. Forward, onward.

weg. Away, beyond.
wieder. Again.
wie oben. As above, as before.

zart. Tenderly, delicately.
ziemlich. Suitable, fit.
zurückhaltend. Slackening in speed.
zurückkehrend zum. Return to, go back to.

Index of Composers

Index of Titles

Index of Forms and Genres

Index to NAWM references in Grout, *History of Western Music*, 3rd ed.